The Battle of NU'UANU
1795

The Battle of NU'UANU *1795*

*An Illustrated Pocket Guide
to the O'ahu Battlefield*

Neil Bernard Dukas

Mutual Publishing

Library of Congress Cataloging-in-Publication Data

Dukas, Neil Bernard.
 The Battle of Nu'uanu, 1795 : an illustrated pocket guide to the O'ahu battlefield
/ Neil B. Dukas.
   p. cm.
 Includes bibliographical references and index.
 ISBN-10: 1-56647-922-3 (softcover : alk. paper)
 ISBN-13: 978-1-56647-922-6
 1. Nu'uanu, Battle of, Oahu, Hawaii, 1795. 2. Battlefields--Hawaii--Honolulu
Region--Guidebooks. I. Title.
 DU627.1.D85 2010
 996.9'02--dc22
                      2010009219

ISBN-10: 1-56647-922-3
ISBN-13: 978-1-56647-922-6

All photos © Neil B. Dukas,
    unless otherwise noted.
Cover photos (bottom left to right)
© Arna Johnson, Elizabeth Helen Moore,
    Arna Johnson
Design by Courtney Young
First Printing, May 2010
Second Printing, June 2014

Mutual Publishing, LLC
1215 Center Street, Suite 210
Honolulu, Hawai'i 96816
Ph: 808-732-1709 / Fax: 808-734-4094
email: info@mutualpublishing.com
www.mutualpublishing.com

Printed in Korea

Contents

Acknowledgements

This guidebook would not have been possible without the support, encouragement and contributions of a great many people. In particular, I would like to thank Francis Ching, Mel Kalahiki, Sr., and Jerry Walker for their heartfelt advice and counsel. You are the very embodiment of the Hawaiian warrior. I would also like to thank Lili and Pono Evensen, John Hart, Arna Johnson, Kepa Lyman, Lesa Moore, Brook Kapūkuniahi Parker, Douglas Peebles, David Phears, Everett Wingert, Matt Lonoikamakahiki W.T. Yim and the staff at the Bishop Museum Library and Archives, Barbara Dunn and the volunteers at the Hawaiian Historical Society, and Dore Minatodani and the staff at University of Hawai'i-Mānoa Hamilton Library, Hawaiian Collection. Last, but not least, thanks to all those who went out of their way to open their doors to me in the spirit of aloha during my many explorations and surveys of the battlefield. You know who you are.

Author's Note

There is actually very little documentation of this crucial battle. The printed word did not take root in Hawai'i until some forty years following the events of 1795. The participants and observers that might have written down the details of their experience in letters or journals were either too troubled with pressing matters in subsequent years to concern themselves with history or their communications have simply been lost to us in the passage of time.

Yet many facets of the battle are indeed well known to us, largely through the strength of Hawaiian oral traditions, both mo'olelo and mele (folk history and traditional chants). To this body of knowledge we can add the supporting journal entries of ensuing visitors to the Islands armed with inquisitive minds and an opportunity to converse with individuals that had some knowledge of events, whether first- or second-hand. As well, there exists the research and interviews conducted by noted nineteenth century historians, of both Native and Missionary origins. Over the last century a number of very respected historians have applied their own interpretations to this material. Not unexpectedly, there are contradictions and inconsistencies in the various accounts—but that need not deter us. Overall these variations tend to be focused on relatively minor matters of detail with little bearing on actual outcome, such as whether a particular protagonist was killed by spear or ball or taken in this or that location. The salient point being that the individual concerned was in fact slain and the battle thus influenced by that particular loss.

Further archaeological study combined with archival research and translation may, in time, alter our understanding of the battle. Meanwhile, this guide to the battlefield is not so much a new interpretation of events as it is a fresh presentation for a contemporary audience, with a little added commentary from the standpoint of the military historian interested in matters of command and control. With these small provisos, any obvious errors or omissions are strictly the responsibility of the author.

"It is appropriate for the new generations of our beloved land to know of certain famous deeds of those persons of old who were well known for their bravery and fearlessness."

—Stephen L. Desha

Introduction

In the opening days of kau wela (the hot or summer season), 1795, a great battle was fought on the Island of Oʻahu between the forces of Kalanikūpule and Kamehameha. We know it today as the "battle of Nuʻuanu," named for the storied valley in which combined Oʻahu and allied forces made a valiant last stand against an invading army from Hawaiʻi.[1] As many as twenty-five thousand warriors participated in the encounter.[2] This is a remarkable number when you consider the entire military establishment for the United States of America was no more than about 3,500 for the same year.[3]

The battle occurred less than twenty years after Cook's voyage of exploration and the reopening of relations with the outside world. Few Western vessels yet visited this isolated quarter of the Pacific.[4] The old religion and kapu restrictions still governed the pulse of Island life. The Polynesian inhabitants, kānaka maoli, a robust and vibrant people well accustomed to warfare, flourished as uncontested masters of their environment.

That same year in far-off Europe, the Prussian philosopher Immanuel Kant published his visionary précis on "Perpetual Peace," while the First Coalition endeavored to cut short the growing reach of Revolutionary France. The man of the hour and "Savior of the Country" was not Napoleon Bonaparte (whose fortunes were still much in doubt), but General Jean-Charles Pichegru. While the Hawaiians under Kamehameha overran Maui, Molokaʻi, and then Oʻahu in a string of knock-out assaults, Pichegru managed to wrest the Netherlands away from allied Dutch, British and Austrian forces before quashing yet another uprising of the *sans-culottes* in Paris. George Washington was still president of the United States and just fifteen stars and stripes adorned the American flag. The tenuous borders of the fledgling republic extended only as far west as Kentucky; the vast territory beyond the juncture of the Ohio and Mississippi rivers (plus Florida) still held in the name of Charles IV of Spain, then too at war with France. The likelihood that these Pacific islands, so far removed from events in

(Elizabeth Helen Moore)

New England, might someday comprise a state of the Union would have seemed to any visitor about as far-fetched as America claiming a title to the Moon.

Affairs in the archipelago, then known to outsiders as the "Sandwich Islands," were focused on an intense competition for leadership that frequently crossed family lines.[5] Nuʻuanu, in a manner of speaking, was the culminating battle in a chain of battles extending back to a war of succession on the "Big Island" beginning in 1782 with the death of the renowned mōʻī (or paramount ruler), Kalaniʻōpuʻu.[6] Sustained by his faith, a combination of good advice, well-crafted coalitions, skill at arms and equal measures of both luck and conviction, Kamehameha rose above the competition to suppress all practical opposition to his rule on the Island of Hawaiʻi.[7]

Beyond the Kohala-Kona shores of his birth, Kamehameha's closest and most serious challenger was Kalanikūpule, heir to a powerful Maui dynasty that dominated most of the remaining archipelago. In 1795 Kalanikūpule ruled from Oʻahu (seized by his late father, the mōʻī Kahikili of Maui, in 1783[8]). The Oʻahu leader, however, maintained an uncertain grip on his widespread dominions.[9] Once before (in the year 1790), he had faced Kamehameha with disastrous results in a battle remembered as Kepaniwai or "Dammed Waters," an allusion to the high price paid by his warriors—the bodies of the dead and dying said to have clogged the torrid mountain stream.[10]

Pursuit of mana, the spiritual life force and quintessential measure of all human accomplishment, virtually guaranteed that these two great rivals, Kamehameha and Kalanikūpule, would one day meet again on the field of battle. The question was when, where and how?

With Kamehameha firmly ensconced as mōʻī of Hawaiʻi, his followers wasted no time amassing a grand fleet in preparation for the inevitable clash.[11] Kalanikūpule, meanwhile, had still to deal with challenges to his own authority. Forced into battle with his uncle, Kāʻeokūlani, the encounter cost him precious manpower, and worse, the backing of a potentially crucial ally in his upcoming confrontation with the ruler of Hawaiʻi.[12]

Kamehameha's massive preparations, meanwhile, cannot have been a secret to Kalanikūpule.[13] Clearly, the Oʻahu leader needed to act, and act swiftly, or find himself on the defensive. Inspired by his victory at ʻAiea, or possibly haunted by the memory of his defeat at ʻĪao Valley, Kalanikūpule chose on this occasion to seize the initiative, preempting his enemy by means of a simple but bloody-minded gambit exploiting both shock and awe. Turning on his unsuspecting English ally, he seized two exceptionally well-armed merchant vessels with the apparent intention of launching a surprise attack on his opponent's fleet while it lay still at anchor and hauled up on the beach.[14] History has judged Kalanikūpule harshly for his duplicity. Nevertheless, it is a hard truth that decisiveness and boldness of action can often turn the tide in battle. Had he succeeded in inflicting serious damage on the assembling fleet, he might very well have forestalled Kamehameha's invasion plans, perhaps forever, altering thereby the course of Hawaiian history and our final assessment of the O'ahu leader. As it happens, the surviving crews of the captured merchantmen got one over on Kalanikūpule, his ambitious scheme ending only in humiliation. In the process, the ill-fated ruler not only lost a quantity of dearly acquired firearms, but his opponent was forewarned and stirred to action. Such are the random fortunes of war.

The Hawaiian fleet set sail from the Big Island sometime in February 1795 with a force conservatively estimated at 10,000. Included in the invasion fleet was a merchant tender, the *Fair American*, commandeered by kaukauali'i (tributary or lesser chiefs) some years earlier and stripped of her guns for use in land-based operations, as well as the first Hawaiian-built vessel of completely Western design, the *Britannia*.[15] Experienced and disciplined fighters, the Hawaiians subdued Maui, then Moloka'i, in a series of well-orchestrated amphibious assaults, subjugating the local populations, living off the land, and bolstering their ranks with newly formed allies. By April, their numbers swollen to about 14,000, Kamehameha and his pūkaua (senior war leaders) were ready for their greatest test—the invasion of O'ahu.

Kalanikūpule, occupying the home ground, was able to call upon 7,000 or so experienced koa (warriors) hastily mustered from allied ali'i on Kaua'i and across his dispersed possessions, plus an additional undefined number of po'ekaua (partially-trained reserves drawn from the common populace). Both sides had access to manufactured arms obtained through trade, alliance, or open conflict, including musket, cannon and cutlass. Although firearms had a definite role to play in the battle, when the time came, opposing forces on O'ahu were outfitted, by and large, with traditional weapons, mostly ihe (spears), newa (clubs), ma'a (slings) and leiomanō (serrated shark-tooth implements), admirably suited for close quarter fighting and the highly mobile tactics of the day.

There is a well-known axiom, '*history is written by the victor*,' and Nu'uanu is certainly no exception.[16] Surviving accounts generally lionize Kamehameha at the expense of Kalanikūpule and his supporters. In these narratives, the Hawaiian forces outsmart and outgun the hapless defenders at every turn. The enemy are swiftly thrown back to the Pali where they meet a debatably glorious, certainly unenviable fate. A careful re-reading and analysis of the events and characters involved, however, is enough to suggest to the military historian that Nuʻuanu may actually have been a much more costly and difficult struggle for the invading force than is generally conceded. War is, after all, a complex undertaking. Many outcomes are possible. If you think it is challenging to organize a gathering of friends and family off-island, imagine what it would take to assemble 10,000 warriors along with family and retainers for an extended campaign under hostile conditions!

Kalanikūpule knew his enemy from intimate experience, had plenty of time to prepare, and with the addition of Kaʻiana, received reinforcements well versed in the trappings of "modern" warfare. So, knowing as we do the upshot of the Hawaiian victory at Nuʻuanu, we are forced to ask ourselves: what indeed went wrong for the combined allied force from Oʻahu, Maui and Kauaʻi? And conversely, what went right for the invading Hawaiians? One way to explore the possibilities is to revisit the battle from the point of view of *the vanquished force*, in this case the Oʻahu defenders. To allow, at least on this occasion, the possibility that although outnumbered and outgunned, they were crafty, intelligent, determined foes—experienced warriors in possession of a plan whose voices have, unfortunately, not survived to share with us their side of the story.

Although rarely recognized as such, the battle of Nuʻuanu surely ranks along with Yorktown, New Orleans, the Alamo, Gettysburg and the Little Bighorn as one of the more momentous clashes of arms to have ever taken place on (what is now) American soil. From a strictly military point of view, the Hawaiian offensive is widely reckoned to be an exemplary amphibious operation, one that any admiral of Kamehameha's day would have remarked upon with great astonishment. Even so, it is important to appreciate that from a contemporary Hawaiian perspective, Nuʻuanu is much more than just another interesting historical fact or tactical problem to be studied. It is a vitally important episode in the life of beloved and respected ancestors, therefore both intensely meaningful and personal.

Whichever way you choose to look at it, Nuʻuanu is unquestionably a formative event in the history of these islands—no less, perhaps, in the historical development of this nation. If the battle had not turned out as it did, Hawai'i might never have been brought into permanent union, much like Samoa remains divided today. There might still be a sovereign government on any one of the major islands, or the Russians still parading on Kaua'i, presenting, therefore, one of the great "ifs" of Pacific history.

Each day, thousands of people travel the roads below Punchbowl and up the Pali Highway. Seldom do they take a moment to contemplate the hallowed ground they are traversing, so hard won (and lost) by the blood and determination of those who have gone before. Curiously few memorials to Nu'uanu exist and precious little of the battlefield is formally preserved on public lands.[17] This guidebook is largely an effort to address that oversight, hopefully stimulating interest in the battle and perhaps some fresh debate.

Although urban sprawl encroaches much of Nu'uanu and the wider battlefield making a detailed study somewhat problematic, the general lay of the land remains unaltered. It is still possible to walk the ground and watch the battle unfold in your mind's eye, to see more or less as Kamehameha and Kalanikūpule did. I encourage you to conduct your own walk/drive study of the battlefield, to take a day or half-day, or perhaps spread your exploration out over a couple of weekends. Apply what you have learned from your reading or family history to what you observe, and then reach your own conclusions. As you retrace the steps of Kalanikūpule, Kamehameha and their pūkaua, you may very well ask yourself: "What would I have done?"

Background

Mana – The Spiritual Essence of a Warrior

Historical reenactor, Kaina Mākua. The pu'u leiomanō in the warrior's hand was crafted by Gordon 'Umi Kai.
(Arna Johnson, Arna Photography)

Hawaiian society flourished for many centuries unimpeded by outside influence. In 1795 Hawaiians still viewed the natural world as a union of opposites, animated by a spiritual force originating with their earliest ancestors and imbuing life, to varying degrees, in all things. In humans, this mana, or life force, manifested itself as different types of intellectual or physical aptitude. This spiritual essence or life force was often an object of competitive ambition, highly prized and sought -after. There were many paths to obtaining or enhancing one's mana, but foremost among them was the way of the warrior, or koa.

Kapu – The Framework for War and Peace

Some means of controlling the flow of mana so that it could be safely directed and preserved was necessary. The Hawaiian answer to this problem was the taboo system, or kapu, an intricate social code designed specifically to balance the dual nature of the universe and manage the flow of mana. In a world devoid of competing ideologies, kapu provided the framework for both war and peace. Good or bad omens, Hawaiians went to war when summoned as a matter of obligation. The penalties for shirking one's duty could be severe in the extreme.

Military Organization and Leadership

The enforcement of kapu laws was carried out by a group of full-time warriors kept within the various courts of ali'i nui. This retinue of professional koa constituted the kernel of Hawai'i's military organization. Each ali'i owed his or her allegiance to a higher authority according to rank. A powerful mō'ī resting atop the hierarchy might exercise direct command over twenty-five hundred such warriors, relying heavily on lower ranking kaukauali'i, or tributary ali'i, to cumulatively supply the remainder of the army in times of war. In this way, an army of some ten thousand well-disciplined and formidable koa could be quickly assembled. Alliances between ali'i or the call-up of semi-trained district militia could substantially swell the number of warriors on the field of battle.

Hawaiian military organization was based on multiples of the number four (forty men were a ka'au, four hundred, a lau, and four thousand, a mano). Once the principal councils of war were convened, the army was led by an ilāmuku (the rough equivalent of a field marshal) or in general terms, a pūkaua. Ali'i commanded military organizations at all levels befitting their rank. There was no precise equivalent to a senior non-commissioned officer corps.

Contact with the West and years of protracted warfare put a new face on the traditional field of battle. By 1795, single combat between individual champions had largely given way to units with specialized functions organized according to skill or capacity. These units were formed at the battalion level (generally two lau), and although likely drawn from chiefly retinues, were structured independently from them. A battalion renowned for its speed, for example, might be expressly designated for the pursuit.

A handful of Europeans and Americans are known to have participated on either side of the battle of Nuʻuanu.[18] Aliʻi purchased firearms in trade or obtained them through open conflict with increasing zeal after 1790. Proficient and adaptable warriors, it is improbable that kānaka maoli still required the services of these individuals to direct them in the use of firearms, a full seven years after their initial introduction.[19] It is more reasonable to attribute the presence of these

Historical reenactor Keliʻiokalani Mākua. ʻElau ihe crafted by Gordon ʻUmi Kai. Mahiole crafted by Raymond Nakama. *(Arna Johnson, Arna Photography)*

foreigners to the tangible advantages derived from their relative social and political separation, written communication skills, and usefulness as interlocutors with other outsiders.[20]

Weapons of War

The major categories of weapons that made up the Hawaiian arsenal included the ihe and pololū (wooden spears of varying lengths), lā'au pālau or newa (cudgels and war clubs), leiomanō (serrated shark-tooth weapons), *ma'a* (slings), and pāhoa (short daggers). Kalanikūpule and his opposite number supplemented their armies with muzzle-loading cannon (mostly small-caliber modified naval carriage guns of four to six pound shot), smoothbore muskets, cutlass, and pistol obtained through trade or conflict from passing merchant vessels. Hawaiians did not make use of the bayonet, famously popular with British forces of the day. It is probable that once engaged in close quarter fighting, the cumbersome and often unreliable muskets were sensibly discarded in favor of traditional weapons. Horses were not introduced until 1803 and therefore had no part in the battle.

Historical reenactor, Chauncey Kalā Lindsey-Asing. Leiomanō crafted by Gordon 'Umi Kai.
(Arna Johnson, Arna Photography)

Estimates vary on how many muskets and cannon were actually employed by either side at the battle of Nu'uanu, certainly more than ever fielded in any previous conflict. Based on the various accounts, it is reasonable to suggest that the Hawaiians paraded 600 (effective) musketeers at Nuʻuanu and perhaps as many as 12 cannon. The latter were apparently given into the charge of John Young.[21] There are no clear estimates for firearms on the Oʻahu side. The Hawaiian guns were especially effective at reducing the perimeter walls at Laʻimi and quite possibly the defensive positions in front of Pūowaina.

There are conflicting accounts concerning the fate of the firearms Kalanikūpule loaded aboard the *Prince Lee Boo* and *Jackal*. The removal of these weapon assets from Kalanikūpule's available arsenal is actually much more significant than their alleged addition to Kamehameha's already substantial holdings.[22]

War Fleet

Amphibious operations were a routine aspect of Hawaiian warfare. In 1795 the average outrigger canoe could accommodate fewer than 30 warriors for inter-island offensives. The great waʻa kaulua (or waʻa kaua) – double-hulled war canoe – with twin "crab-claw" sails were generally limited to chiefly retinues. It was not until after Kamehameha's victory on Oʻahu and establishment of a large naval yard at Kawaihae (1796-1802) that Kamehameha's fleet came to include peleleu in any serious numbers.[23] Peleleu were exceptionally large, sturdy, and maneuverable canoes of essentially Hawaiian design but incorporating Western-style sails. A swivel gun was sometimes mounted on the foredeck. Kamehameha's invasion fleet also included a small schooner, the *Britannia*, the first completely Western-style vessel built in Hawaiʻi. It was the *Britannia* that transported the Hawaiian ordnance under Young's care for the offensive at Nuʻuanu.

Battle Dress

Most men went to war wearing only a narrow malo (loincloth), tucked in and girded slightly higher above the hips than usually positioned on the body. Musketeers would sling a cartouche belt and powder horn or hue (gourd flask) over one shoulder. Highly skilled warriors proficient in lua, the ancient Hawaiian art of combat, might slick down their bodies and reject all forms of garb to thwart an enemy's handhold. The ordinary ranks of some units adopted a turban-like head wrap fashioned from kapa, which served to cushion a blow and aid in the identification of comrades. Ali'i wore ornate helmets called mahiole that were sometimes surmounted by an impressive crest, or haka, and majestic 'ahu 'ula, (feather cloaks). The patterns were unique to the wearer and the length indicative of rank. In the heat of battle these distinctive garments served to pinpoint the location of leadership and to rally warriors.

Women in Battle

In general, women accompanied their husbands on campaign, carrying food and water, aiding the wounded, and offering encouragement from the sidelines. There appears to have been no specific "taboo" against women participating in battle, especially when things were going badly and every pair of willing hands was valued for their contribution. Female ali'i nui could command troops, of course, by virtue of their rank, although in practice this rarely applied outside the more or less routine police functions of court. Still, references to "noted" female fighters in Hawaiian oral traditions are not all that unusual.[24] There are various accounts of some female ali'i proficient in the use of firearms participating in the battle of Nu'uanu, notably in the encounters at La'imi and Pū'iwa.[25]

Time Frame

The date of the battle has been estimated at late April, 1795. Various attempts at pinpointing the precise date for the battle have thus far proven unsuccessful. Circumstantial evidence suggests that the Hawaiian beachhead was attained somewhere close to the last week of April, the opening of hostilities about three days later, and mopping-up operations continuing into the early part of May.

Designation – The Battle of Nu'uanu

Sometimes called the "battle of Nu'uanu Pali." Other traditional names include:
- Kaleleka'anae ("the leaping mullet")

- Ka'uwa'u pali ("clawed off the cliff"[26])

These names allude to the final desperate action at the Pali. Most students of military history prefer the more encompassing title, "battle of Nu'uanu," since it provides scope for all the contributing actions, including those below Punchbowl, lower Nu'uanu, and at Kahuailanawai.[27]

Major Protagonists

Attacking force – Hawai'i

- Kamehameha – mō'ī, Island of Hawai'i

Defending allied force(s) – O'ahu

- Kalanikūpule – mō'ī, O'ahu, Moloka'i, Lāna'i, Maui, and Kaho'olawe[28]

- Unknown individual – representing Kaumuali'i, mō'ī of Kaua'i and Ni'ihau

- Ka'iana (Keawe-Ka'iana-a-'Ahu'ula) – ali'i nui, Kaua'i and Hawai'i[29]

Deployment of Principal Forces

Attacking force – Hawai'i (12,000)[30]

Kāhala/Wai'alae location: 3 divisions of approximately 300 canoes each, Ke'eaumoku commanding:
- The Huelokū – 1 mano, 1 lau (approximate total 4,400)

- The Hunalele – 1 mano, 1 lau (approximate total 4,400)

- The Kaikaoa – 2 lau (800)

Waikīkī: One division of approximately 300 canoes, Kamehameha/Kekūhaupi'o commanding:
- The 'Ālapa – 6 lau (2,400)

Defending allied force(s) – O'ahu (9,000)

Pūowaina/Nu'uanu combined divisions, Kalanikūpule/Ka'iana commanding:[31]
- Indeterminate organization – 2 mano, 2 lau, 5 ka'au (approximate total 9,000 including a hapamano of 2,000 supplied by Ka'iana[32])

The War of Unification – Its Origins and Conditions

"The site of ancient kings of pure descent, and with the reputation besides of great natural fertility, O'ahu was destined to be a prized object" says noted scholar and ethnographer, Marshall Sahlins.[33]

Seized by Kahikili of Maui in 1783, O'ahu provided the power base for his son, Kalanikūpule. The remaining possessions (Lāna'i, Moloka'i and Maui proper) fell loosely to Kalanikūpule in 1794 following the defeat of his uncle and foremost internal rival for supremacy, Kā'eokūlani of Kaua'i. With the defeat of Kā'eo, Kaua'i and Ni'ihau, although independent, fell within the Maui-O'ahu sphere of influence.

On the death of the mō'ī Kalani'ōpu'u in 1782, Kamehameha was famously charged with the care of the god Kūka'ilimoku (Kū – snatcher of islands). Kamehameha took this sacred obligation seriously, evincing an early desire to expand the reach of his authority. Once his rule was consolidated on Hawai'i, he came quickly into conflict with the Maui dynasty.[34]

Following back-to-back defeats of Maui forces at ʻĪao in 1790, and a combined Kauaʻi and Maui force in the battle of Kepuwahaʻulaʻula, March 1791, the allies established and maintained a large standing army on the Hawaiʻi-facing shores of Maui. The sustained effort required to keep up this force severely strapped the agricultural resources of the extended Maui kingdom, furthermore, hampering Kalanikūpule's ability to participate in a *de facto* arms race with Hawaiʻi.[35]

The Battle – Causal Factors

The final confrontation between rivals Kamehameha and Kalanikūpule might have unfolded in any number of ways, but two things combined to bring them to battle on this occasion. The first was Kalanikūpule's victory over his uncle at the battle of ʻAiea, or Kukiʻiahu, in December 1794. This had the effect of removing Kāʻeokūlani from consideration on Maui, where his forces and leadership might have otherwise provided a continued deterrent against Kamehameha's aggression. The second was Kalanikūpule's botched attempt at purloining two well-armed merchant vessels. The escaped crews of these ships provided Kamehameha with invaluable intelligence on the intentions and disposition of Kalanikūpule's forces. Moreover, it was abundantly clear that he had lost the military backing of the English merchant vessels and their masters, which would have assuredly vexed Kamehameha's invasion plans for Oʻahu.

Historical reenactor, Keliʻiokalani Mākua.
Newa crafted by Raymond Nakama.
(Arna Johnson, Arna Photography)

Historical reenactor, Fred Peleke Flores. Ihe laumeki crafted by Gordon 'Umi Kai. *(Arna Johnson, Arna Photography.)*

A Chant

Without a written language to transmit social history and cultural values, mele (an ancient form of poetry recited as a chant) took on a heightened significance in Hawai'i. "In the elaborate system of ancient days, life was a continuous ceremony and there was an appropriate mele for every occasion."[36] The Hawaiian tradition of mele survives, as exemplified in this chant commemorating the battle of Nu'uanu composed by the late kumu (teacher) and community leader Pilahi Paki. She notes, "Hawai'i can be found, in its true essence, by understanding the oral expressions voiced by the people of ancient times."[37]

Warriors were many,
In the days of old.
Splendid men, tall and broad,
Of muscles firm, and sinewy arms,
Their golden-brown skin
Glowing clearly as sunshine.

Here, in the Valley of Nu'uanu,
When the winds blow steadily,
Sometimes calm and often wild,
Those bronze god-men fought
Under the mighty chief,
The first Kamehameha.

Kamehameha the Lonely,
Famed warrior and king.

The Battle began when marching men
Landed canoes at Sandy Beach,
(Ke-awa-luku, the native name

Of that beckoning, lovely beach).
Their marching feet climbed
To the Pali Pass...

Imagine the Valley
As it was that day...

When foot-trails straggled
Through verdure dense,
Growing among giant forest-trees.

There were scattered houses
Of Pili-grass,
Man-built temples,
Heiau of stones
Where hand-carved gods
Mounted the walls,
and gazed so wordlessly
Upon the silent, marching spearmen.
In mind's eye, imagine

Those warriors, and army,
Storming the temples
And rocky walls,
Defying bravely the great Unknown
Of those fiercely-glaring gods!

That was the way
Nu'uanu was conquered,
Temple by temple,
And god after god,

Until, the last, O'ahu's army,
Led by the heavenly
Ka-lani-ku-pule,
Could no longer defend
The people and land.

"Retreat! Brave men,
Run for your lives!"
Those were the words
Of that noble king
To his army of bronze men.
Obedient, ever, to his command,
The army fled blindly
Into the hills.
Fleetly, in sorrow,
They strove ever upward.

Then, at the Pass, behold
Their surprise!

When, caught in Nature's
Forgotten trap,
They saw no place to turn,
No way to go back
From the steep cliff-edge,
Rim-of-death, there, confronting!

Behind them, the death-spears,
Pointed up toward them,
Blocking return, on left

And on right.
Their only escape
The depths ahead...
They leaped...
Thus ended the strife.

History records
That sacrifice made,
By those bronze warriors
Of long ago,
Who leapt to Death,
Unconquered still,
By all the awed enemy
At Kahili Hill.

Warriors and spears,
All disappeared
From the Cliff-edge there,
Where the Trade Winds blow,
and perfumed verdure
Still hides their graves.

Today that age-old story
Is told in a ballad-song.
You may have heard it,
Sun loudly and long:

"King Kamehameha
Conqueror of the islands,
Became a famous hero one day.
He fought a mighty army
And pushed it over the Pali,
Auwe! Ke Aloha, e!"

—"Battle of Nuuanu" from Pilahi Paki,
Legends of Hawaii, Oahu's Yesterday.

Battlefield Study

Phase 1 – The Beachhead

Suggested Vantage Point: Lē'ahi (Diamond Head Crater)
[see street map on page 15]

- From Diamond Head Road take the entrance road up to Diamond Head State Monument.

- Turn left into the small parking lot located just *in front* of the tunnel entrance. Free short-term parking.

- View from rail: Maunalua Bay (Kāhala/Wai'alae coast to Koko Head).

- **Note:** There is a fee for parking inside the crater.

Kamehameha landing at O'ahu. Renowned artist and historian Herb Kawainui Kāne's depiction of Hawaiian peleleu rounding the headlands off Waikīkī.
("Kamehameha Landing at Oahu" © 2009 Herb Kawainui Kāne)

HAWAIIAN INVASION ROUTE
FEBRUARY – APRIL 1795

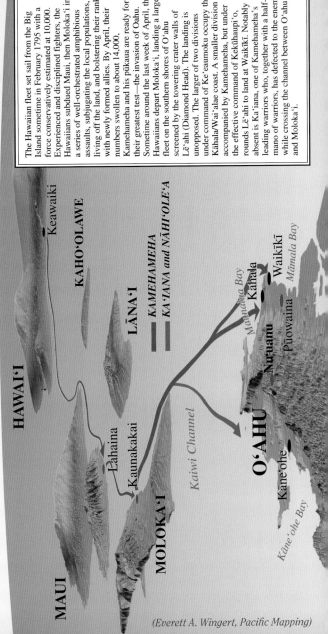

The Hawaiian fleet set sail from the Big Island sometime in February 1795 with a force conservatively estimated at 10,000. Experienced and disciplined fighters, the Hawaiians subdued Maui, then Moloka'i in a series of well-orchestrated amphibious assaults, subjugating the local populations, living off the land, and bolstering their ranks with newly formed allies. By April, their numbers swollen to about 14,000, Kamehameha and his pūkaua are ready for their greatest test—the invasion of Oahu. Sometime around the last week of April, the Hawaiians depart Moloka'i, landing a large fleet on the southern shores of O'ahu screened by the towering crater walls of Lē'ahi (Diamond Head). The landing is unopposed. The larger of two divisions under command of Ke'eaumoku occupy the Kāhala/Wai'alae coast. A smaller division accompanied by Kamehameha, but under the effective command of Kekūhaupi'o, rounds Lē'ahi to land at Waikīkī. Notably absent is Ka'iana, one of Kamehameha's leading warriors who, together with a half-mano of warriors, has defected to the enemy while crossing the channel between O'ahu and Moloka'i.

HAWAI'I

Keawaiki

KAHO'OLAWE

LĀNA'I

▌▌ KAMEHAMEHA
▌▌ KA'IANA and NĀHI'OLE'A

MAUI

Lāhaina

Kaunakakai

MOLOKA'I

Kaiwi Channel

Maunalua Bay

Kāhala

Waikīkī

Māmala Bay

Nu'uanu

Pūowaina

O'AHU

Kāne'ohe

Kāne'ohe Bay

(Everett A. Wingert, Pacific Mapping)

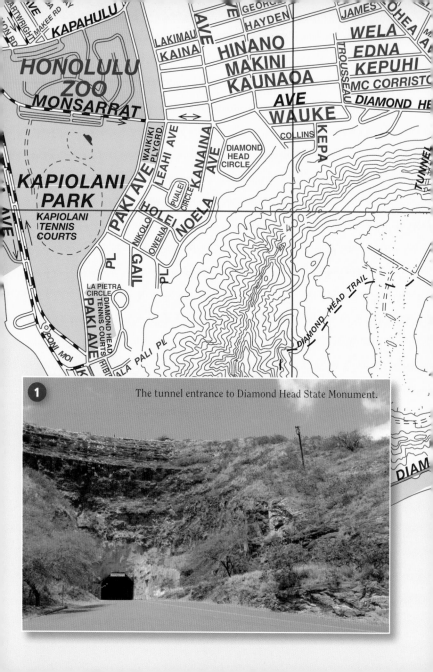

The tunnel entrance to Diamond Head State Monument.

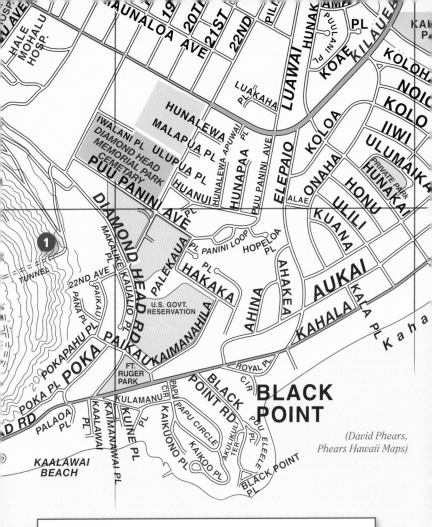

(David Phears,
Phears Hawaii Maps)

Legend for Street Maps*

1 Phases of battle   **A** Vicinity of noted sites

*Note: Contemporary photographs of sites use the same lettered or numbered symbol to aid in identification.

Sometime around the last week of April 1795, the Hawaiians depart Moloka'i, landing a large fleet on the southern shores of O'ahu screened by the towering crater walls of Lē'ahi (Diamond Head). The landing is unopposed.[38] The larger of two divisions under command of Ke'eaumoku occupy the Kāhala/Wai'alae coast. A smaller division accompanied by Kamehameha, but under the effective command of Kekūhaupi'o, rounds Lē'ahi to land at Waikīkī.[39]

Notably absent is Ka'iana (Keawe-Ka'iana-a-'Ahu'ula), one of Kamehameha's leading warriors. A falling out with Kamehameha's closest advisors has led to Ka'iana's exclusion from a council of war at Kaunakakai. Bittered and fearing for his life, Ka'iana veers toward the windward, or Ko'olau, side of O'ahu together with a half-mano of warriors while crossing the channel between O'ahu and Moloka'i.[40] Together with his supporters, Ka'iana defects to Kalanikūpule.

Without any clear knowledge of Kamehameha's intentions, Kalanikūpule decides not to oppose the Hawaiian landing along a broad front, opting instead to concentrate his forces, fortifying positions around the base of Pūowaina and at Nu'uanu. The Hawaiians, for their part, have selected the ideal beachhead, wide enough to easily accommodate hundreds of canoes and campfires. The waters off Waikīkī can accommodate the larger vessels in the fleet, but perhaps more importantly, control of Waikīkī also means guaranteed access to fresh water, fishponds, and the sacred places flanking Lē'ahi. With Lē'ahi ridgeline secured, the Hawaiians have clear observation in all directions and can consolidate at their leisure without fear of surprise or harassment. They can also maintain continuous contact between their divisions at Waikīkī and Kāhala/Wai'alae.

No doubt, the unexpected loss of Ka'iana together with a significant cache of firearms requires some rethinking and planning. The poor conditions on O'ahu—owing to years of neglect and harsh demands on agriculture—make foraging for supplies a troublesome and time-consuming task for the invading force.[41] The Hawaiians take time, perhaps three to four days, to consolidate their position, regroup, resupply and reconnoiter.

Once ready, the Hawaiians set out at first light across the open coastal plain of the Kona district, advancing in three lines, the 'Ālapa

Approaching Lēʻahi (Diamond Head) from the direction of Kaiwi Channel.
Photo by Tai Sing Loa, 1924. *(Hawaiian Historical Society photo)*

View from Diamond Head State Monument past Kāhala toward Koko Head.

An aerial view of Lēʻahi (Diamond Head) with Kūpikipikiʻo (Black Point) in the fore-ground, the beachhead for the Hawaiian invasion. *(Douglas Peebles Photography)*

division from Waikīkī combining with the three divisions from Kāha-la/Waiʻalae. Traveling a distance of about five miles, they halt just in advance of the allied screening force.[42]

A NOTE ON THE VARIOUS NARRATIONS

Some (rare) accounts of the landing include Waimānalo or Sandy Beach, but the majority simply state "from Waiʻalae to Waikīkī." "Waiʻalae" is best inter-preted as a direction (much as ʻEwa is used to indicate direction), rather than a precise location.

According to one narration, fearing Kaʻiana might attempt a surprise attack, Kamehameha orders Young to position three guns covering the landing.[43]

O'AHU

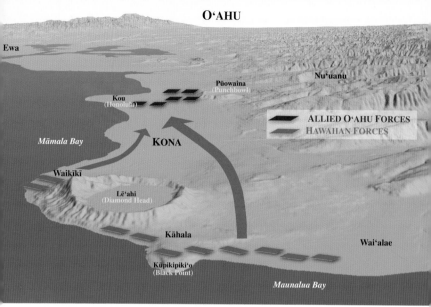

Ewa

Nu'uanu

Pūowaina
(Punchbowl)

Kou
(Honolulu)

KONA

Māmala Bay

Waikīkī

Lē'ahi
(Diamond Head)

Kāhala

Wai'alae

Kūpikipiki'o
(Black Point)

Maunalua Bay

ALLIED O'AHU FORCES
HAWAIIAN FORCES

(Everett A. Wingert, Pacific Mapping)

Lē'ahi pinnacle (Diamond Head) as viewed from Kapi'olani Park in Waikīkī.

Phase 2 – The Screen

Suggested Vantage Point: Thomas Square
[see street map below]

- Community park at intersection of South King Street and Victoria Street. Street parking.

Like Harold Godwinson after the battle of Stamford Bridge (1066), Kalanikūpule defeats his uncle and rival, Kāʻeokūlani, only to find an even more formidable opponent waiting for him on the shore. But

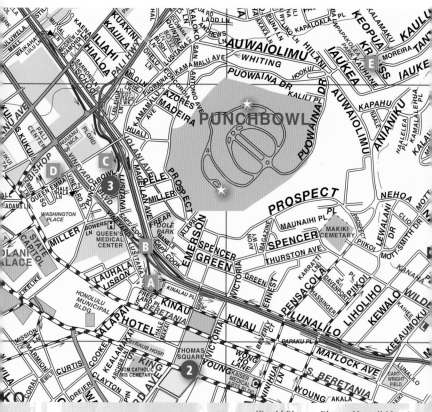

(David Phears, Phears Hawaii Maps)

The view from Moana Hotel in Waikīkī toward Punchbowl. Famed for its freshwater, Waikīkī could still boast vast taro fields in 1900; the fishponds were no longer in much evidence. *(Photo by Ray Jerome Baker, circa 1900. Hawaiian Historical Society)*

Thomas Square, famous for its part in the events marking the restoration of Hawaiian sovereignty in 1843, today is a popular site for community gatherings. The vicinity of Kalanikūpule's defensive screen.

A skirmish employing traditional weapons.
(Illustration © 2009 Brook Kapūkuniahi Parker)

he has had ample time to ready himself. The allies form a protective screen in the vicinity of where Thomas Square and McKinley High School stand today. The old religion, warrior traditions, sense of destiny and loyalty were not diminished on this day. The opposing warriors face one another more or less as they have for centuries, psyched and prepared for battle.

First contact provides the opportunity for both parties to engage in formalities, including supplication and ritual taunts. The skirmish has a three-fold purpose: to intimidate, to probe for strengths and weaknesses, and to obtain sacrificial victims. Kalanikūpule has a fourth purpose. The screening force masks his defenses and, as the screen pulls back, deliberately draws the enemy toward his hardened positions.

According to one school of thought, Kalanikūpule deliberately withdraws his troops toward the narrow valley of Nuʻuanu where cannon pre-positioned atop the flanking ridgelines await the unsuspecting Hawaiians, in effect, luring the invaders into a trap or ambush.

On the other hand, Kalanikūpule, who was seriously burned at ʻĪao Valley, can well be forgiven for not wishing to repeat that terrible mistake. Instead he relies on hardened defenses dominating the high ground *well in advance* of Nuʻuanu and furnishing them with as much firepower as he can possibly spare. Moreover, at ʻĪao Kalanikūpule managed a successful escape over the pass while his dedicated forces held the mouth of the valley. Nuʻuanu, with its numerous heiau (places of worship often built upon heavy stone platforms), suggests a similar opportunity should the mōʻī's forward defenses fail.

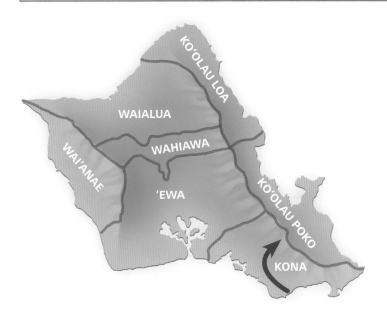

The Moku of Oʻahu (circa 1795) illustrating the Hawaiian advance across the *ʻokana,* or district, of Kona, Oʻahu.

Phase 3 – The First Line of Defense

Suggested Vantage Point: Five Sites (A-E)
[see street map on page 20]

- There are five battle-related sites located around the base of Punchbowl (labeled A through E).

- **Note:** These sites can be viewed individually or conveniently studied from the top of Punchbowl (see section on Pūowaina or "Punchbowl" on page 38).

The two armies meet in full-on battle at the foot of Pūowaina (Punchbowl Crater).[44] The allied defenders, reinforced perhaps by some of Kaʻiana's warriors, are well entrenched, employing several heiau as forward bastions or redoubts. These are prepared defenses.

Although the particulars of the fighting in front of Pūowaina have not come down to us in any great detail, it is more than likely the defenders have established gun emplacements atop these heiau. The first position to receive a direct assault by the Hawaiians is Kānelāʻau heiau, located somewhere near the intersection of today's Alapaʻi and Kīnaʻu streets. The other three bastions come into play one at a time as the Hawaiian vanguard, and then the main body, pivots around to face the defenders.

Arranged in a rough semi-circle, the fortified heiau divide the attentions of the attacking force, luring the enemy into a shared killing ground.[45] "Here the battle raged the fiercest," records Emma Metcalf Nukuina.[46]

Today, the area from Punchbowl to Diamond Head is one of the most densely populated areas in the Pacific.

A NOTE ON THE VARIOUS NARRATIONS

The most frequently-cited versions of the battle describe the Hawaiians quickly bisecting the allied front below Pūowaina, isolating the defensive positions into separate and indefensible halves. This phase of the battle then becomes a simple matter of divide and conquer.

From behind their redoubts the allies would naturally attempt to employ both musket and cannon against targets of opportunity. This aligns with accounts suggesting that the Hawaiian guns were not present during the early part of the battle, but were kept at sea until seizure of the harbor at Kou (Honolulu) could be affected. If this is indeed the case, direct assaults on the fortified heiau might have incurred significant casualties, perhaps the only serious losses suffered by the Hawaiians during the entire battle.

If prior practice is any indication, the defenders resort to sallies once their powder runs dry, advancing from their positions to employ traditional close quarter fighting techniques and then rotating back to the redoubts to alternate with fresh troops as required. With the advantage of high ground and well-prepared positions, the defense of Pūowaina can thus be sustained for some hours, even against a larger force.

The view from Punchbowl to Diamond Head circa 1890s looking across what was once known as Kona, Oʻahu. *(Davey Photo Company, Hawaiian Historical Society photo)*

Punchbowl Crater, which was formerly known as Pūowaina. In 1795 it was an ancient hill of sacrifice. Today, it is the location of the National Memorial Cemetery of the Pacific. The allies established their first line of defence at the foot of Pūowaina. Homes blanket Pacific Heights and Pauoa Valley at the rear left of photo. *(Douglas Peebles Photography)*

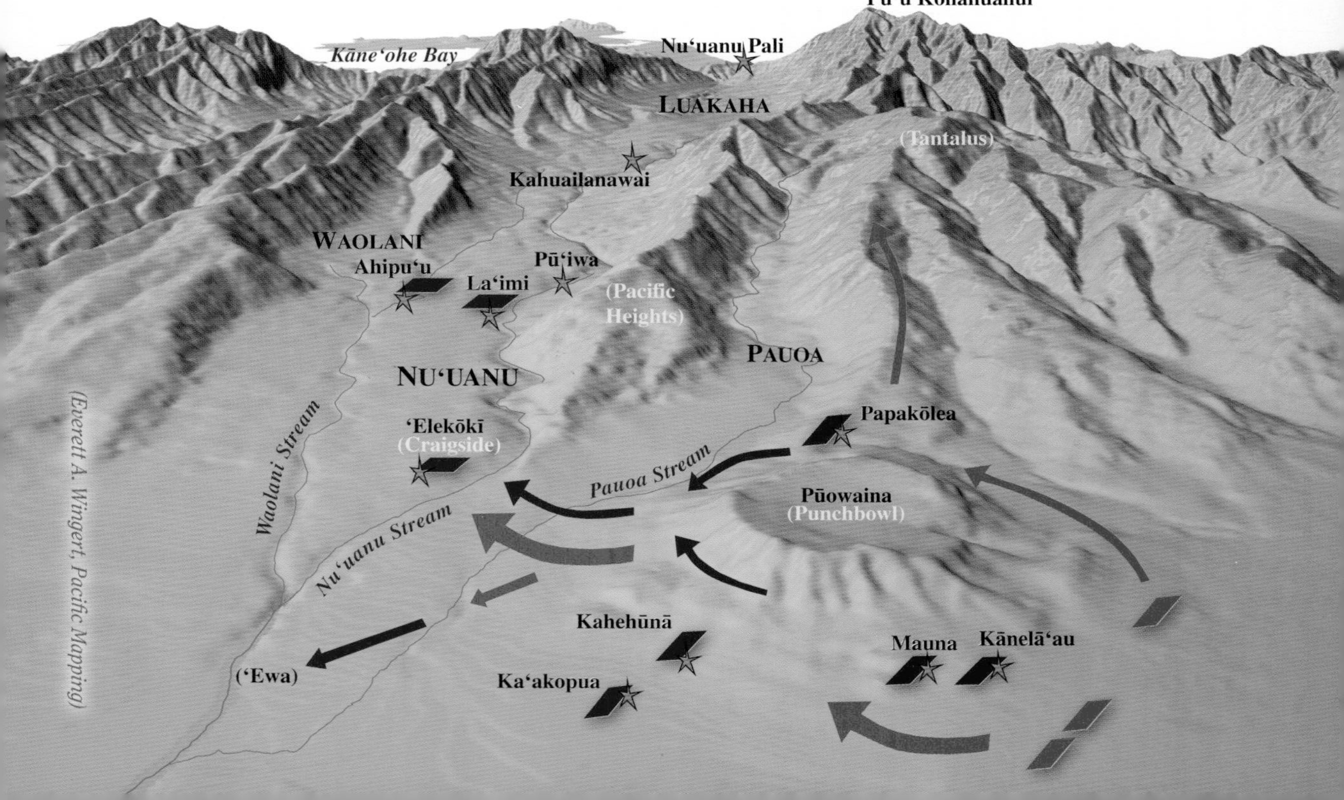

Pu'u Kōnāhuanui

Nu'uanu Pali

Nu'uanu Pali

LUAKAHA

(Tantalus)

Kahuailanawai

Pū'iwa

La'imi

(Pacific Heights)

Papakōlea

PAUOA

Pūowaina (Punchbowl)

WAOLANI
Ahipu'u

NU'UANU

'Elekōkī (Craigside)

Pauoa Stream

Kahehūnā

Mauna Kānela'au

Ka'akopua

Nu'uanu Stream

Waolani Stream

('Ewa)

(Everett A. Wingert, Pacific Mapping)

A FORMER KĀNELĀʻAU HEIAU

Suggested Vantage Point:

- The intersection of Alapaʻi Street and Kīnaʻu Street below the Lunalilo Freeway. Street parking.

Located on the defender's forward left flank. Scene of the first major combat of the battle and some of the bloodiest two-way fighting.

The intersection of Alapaʻi Street and Kīnaʻu Street below the Lunalilo Freeway. Vicinity of the former Kānelāʻau heiau and scene of some of the bloodiest fighting.

An aliʻi kaua with musket and
accoutrements, circa 1795.
*(Illustration © 2009
Brook Kapūkuniahi Parker)*

Short Land Pattern Musket or "Brown Bess." Introduced in 1769, the Short Land Pattern model smoothbore flintlock remained in service with the British Army until the 1790s. Untested knock-offs were routinely traded in the Pacific by unscrupulous merchant captains in exchange for supplies. These weapons were typically fabricated from substandard materials and often carried counterfeit hallmarks. Even under the best conditions they fouled quickly and misfired or exploded with repeated use, posing almost as great a hazard to their handler as they did to the enemy. Hawaiians did not make use of the bayonet that normally accompanied the musket. The cumbersome firearms were most likely discarded in favor of traditional weapons during close quarter fighting. *(Photo by Ross McKenzie, Royal Military College of Canada)*

B FORMER MAUNA HEIAU[47]

Suggested Vantage Point:

- Just above Queen's Medical Center, near Lusitana Street and Lauhala Street.[48] Street parking.

Located on the defender's center left of line.

Vicinity of Mauna (or Mana) heiau just above Queen's Medical Center near Lusitana Street and Lauhala Street.

C FORMER KAHEHŪNĀ HEIAU

Suggested Vantage Point:

- Vicinity of Royal School at Punchbowl Street and Lusitana Street. Street parking.

Located on the defender's center right of line.

Royal School and Central Middle School (vicinity of Kahehūnā and Kaʻakopua heiau) viewed from the observation point atop Punchbowl.

The original Royal School.
(Photo by H.L. Chase, circa 1868-1872. Hawaiian Historical Society photo)

Royal School, Punchbowl Street and Lusitana Street.
Vicinity of the former Kahehūnā heiau.

D FORMER KAʻAKOPUA HEIAU

Suggested Vantage Point:

- Vicinity of Central Middle School at Queen Emma Street and Vineyard Boulevard. Street parking.

Located on the defender's forward right flank.

Central Middle School, Queen Emma Street and Vineyard Boulevard. Vicinity of the former Kaʻakopua heiau, and later, Keōua Hale, the royal palace of Princess Ruth Keʻelikōlani.

View of Pūowaina from the pedestrian overpass adjacent to Central Middle School.

View toward Punchbowl. Note Keōua Hale at left. Photo circa 1890s.
(Hawaiian Historical Society photo)

Keōua Hale was the royal palace of Princess Ruth Ke'elikōlani, completed in 1884. Now the site of Central Middle School. Photo circa 1890s. *(Hawaiian Historical Society photo)*

E PAPAKŌLEA

Suggested Vantage Point:

- Papakōlea Community Park. Located at the intersection of Tantalus Drive and Kauhane Street. Street parking. **Watch for children at play!**

Papakōlea occupies the "saddle" behind Pūowaina, connecting the crater to the base of the ridge heading up to Tantalus. Standing atop Punchbowl, it is easy to see how critical the defense of Papakōlea must have been to the overall allied strategy. Without control of Papakōlea the defensive positions in front of Pūowaina are open to attack from behind and the planned withdrawl route up Nu'uanu Valley imperiled. Papakōlea's retention, in fact, is so fundamental to their security that Kalanikūpule and his pūkaua must certainly have taken major steps to defend it. The Hawaiians eventually manage to infiltrate Papakōlea, but how? Is it through some form of subterfuge?[49] Perhaps due to a

E

A view of Pauoa from atop Punchbowl. Papakōlea is just to the right of frame.

simple oversight on the part of the allied commanders? Or worse, negligence or treachery? We will likely never know what actually happened at Papakōlea, one of the more intriguing events of the battle.[50]

What can well be imagined is that with Papakōlea in enemy hands, time is now of the essence. The allies have no choice but to abandon their positions in front of Pūowaina and to move in haste to the mouth of Pauoa Valley. Failing to do so will allow the attackers, now pouring over the saddle at Papakōlea, to get behind them and cut off their only escape route; in effect, ending the battle then and there.

Since the Hawaiians, we know, are unable to seize Nuʻuanu before the allies can secure it for themselves, the allied blocking maneuver at Pauoa must be considered a success. With the bulk of their forces

The "backside" of Pūowaina taken from Pauoa.

removed to the lower reaches of Nuʻuanu and disaster at least tempo-
rarily averted, the allies can then withdraw their force from Pauoa and
relocate to prepared positions midway up Nuʻuanu. The fight, it would
seem, is still far from decided.

Undeterred by this minor setback, the Hawaiians shrewdly dis-
patch a flanking division up the unprotected ridgeline toward Puʻu
ʻŌhiʻa (Tantalus). With the probable assistance of someone with intimate knowledge of the trails, it is only a matter of time to see the
flanking division over Pauoa Flats and down the back of Nuʻuanu.

The allied senior command, all experienced and capable warriors, is still very much intact at this point. While the fighting along this stretch may very well have been close and intense, there is no reason to suppose that the allied withdrawal from Pūowaina is anything but orderly.

It is commonly suggested that the objective of the flanking maneuver conducted by the Hawaiians, was inspired by intelligence revealing the presence of allied cannon on the ridgeline above Nuʻuanu. This possibility is a matter of considerable debate as the sources are unclear on the issue and the practicalities of placing guns on the ridge more than a little problematic (see discussion of the "Pali Notches" on page 58).

SUGGESTED VANTAGE POINT FOR EASY VIEWING:

Pūowaina or "Punchbowl" (National Memorial Cemetery of the Pacific)

- U.S. Armed Forces cemetery located in an extinct volcanic crater. Enter from Pūowaina Drive. The cemetery has formal hours. No entrance or parking fees.

- Ancient place of sacrifice and final resting place for more than 30,000 soldiers and aliʻi.

- (✷) From the makai (ocean) side lookout or observation point, view sites A–D, above. Also, ʻEwa views (i.e., in the direction of leeward Oʻahu) and Diamond Head.

- (✷) From the mauka (inland) side. Views toward Pauoa, Nuʻuanu (Site F, below), and Papakōlea (Site E, above). **Please be respectful of the monuments while crossing cemetery grounds.**

Sometime during the allied withdrawal from Pūowaina, a small allied force under Kaomealani departs the battle in the direction of ʻEwa, pursued by the Hawaiian pūkaua, Nahili.[51]

A NOTE ON THE VARIOUS NARRATIONS

It is not unusual to come across accounts of the battle that portray Kaomealani's force as "fleeing" the fight after the Hawaiians have managed to isolate the allied defensive positions in front of Pūowaina.

Since there is no corroborating evidence either way and Kaomealani is not here to defend his actions, it is fair to suggest that this was not a rout, but a calculated tactical decision aimed at drawing off a sizable body of attacking forces. Nahili was a respected commander and his removal from the immediate theater employing just a small amount of bait would have substantially bettered Kalanikūpule's odds of success at Nuʻuanu. The opportunity for a ploy such as this would have been evident to any experienced commander.

It is also possible that the Hawaiians were eventually able to bring their guns to bear on the allied positions below Pūowaina and that this, either alone or in combination with the action at Papakōlea, contributed to the collapse of the forward positions. This remains a point of speculation, however, as there is nothing in the surviving accounts to suggest an early deployment of Hawaiian ordnance.

Phase 4 – The Tactical Withdrawal/Second Line of Defense

Suggested Vantage Point: Five Sites (F-J)
[see street map on page 41]

- There are five battle-related sites located in Nuʻuanu Valley, labeled F through J.

The second line of the allied defense was the ahupuaʻa of Nuʻuanu (commonly referred to as "Nuʻuanu Valley"), located mauka (inland) of the harbor at Kou (Honolulu).[52] The valley stretches upward at a steady incline from the coast, eventually penetrating deep into the towering Koʻolau range. Its walls are steep, often razor-backed, and difficult to traverse throughout much of their length. The flanking ridgelines are separated by about a mile at the lower reaches, narrowing to a tight pass or gap at the head of the valley. The gap, now generally known as "Nuʻuanu Pali," sits at an elevation of about 1,200 feet, some five or

Looking ʻEwa from Punchbowl observation point. Kaomealani headed in this direction with a small force pursued by Nahili after the collapse of the Pūowaina defences.

six miles inland of Honolulu. The winds at the Pali are fierce and the rains are frequent.[53]

Nuʻuanu has always maintained a special place in Hawaiian culture and society, for reasons that extended well beyond its agreeable microclimate. It was a center for agriculture in addition to providing the main trunk for trade and communication between windward and leeward Oʻahu. In 1795 breadfruit, noni, bananas, yams, sweet potatoes, sugarcane, coconut, screwpine and kī (ti plant) might have been found growing in Nuʻuanu. The ridgelines and higher elevations might still have supported forests of ʻōhiʻa, koa and ʻiliahi (sandalwood).[54] The valley has a much deeper and profoundly spiritual significance as well. Nestled within its middle reaches, in the secluded salient of Waolani, lies the legendary home of Wākea and his wife, Papahaumea, traditional forebearers of the kānaka maoli. In 1795, Kawaʻluna, a heiau seeped in mana of the most powerful sort and a complex of lesser heiau occupied Waolani.[55]

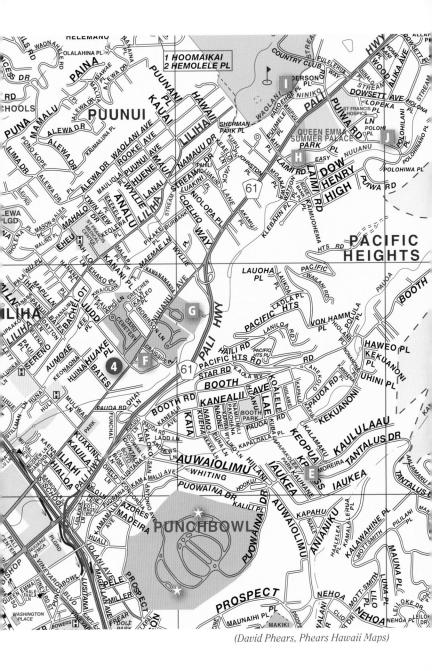

(David Phears, Phears Hawaii Maps)

At Ahipuʻu and Laʻimi the ancient Oahuans built strongholds to protect their sacred sites. For countless generations a beacon fire at Haipu atop the Pauoa ridge warned the kapu guards of any approaching threat.[56] It was here, at Ahipuʻu and Laʻimi, that Kalanikūpule, with reinforcements provided by Kaʻiana, prepared his second line of defense.

F ʻELEKŌKĪ

Suggested Vantage Point:

- Between South Judd Street and Craigside Place off Nuʻuanu Avenue. Street parking.

Homes fill the mouth of Pauoa Valley (foreground). According to one school of thought, Kalanikūpule's retiring forces attempted to withdraw up this valley, but were interdicted by Kamehameha's flanking division crossing over Papakōlea. Rebuffed, the defenders fled over the ridge to Nuʻuanu where they established a new line of defense at ʻElekōkī (left of frame, located just beyond the line of the Pali Highway, in the vicinity of the Craigside apartment building).

Following their retreat from Pūowaina and Pauoa, the allies moved rapidly, but in order up Nuʻuanu, with the Hawaiians hard at their heels. The allies fight a typical staged withdrawal in contact, one force holding while the other continues back to establish a new position before relieving the forward force, in a sort of leap-frog fashion.

ʻElekōkī, located within the former ʻili of Kawānanakoa, can no longer be found on most maps.[57] It was situated on the forward slope where the Craigside development now stands. A terrace or heiau wall once ran near the makai side of what is now Judd Street. It was here

Arial view of Nuʻuanu from the direction of Honolulu. 1929 photo by G.R. Hayman, 11th Photo Section, U.S. Army Air Corps. *(Hawaiian Historical Society photo)*

Craigside, at Nu'uanu Avenue and South Judd Street. The vincinity of 'Elekōkī in the former 'ili of Kawānanakoa. The allies, holding the higher ground, conducted a staged withdrawl up Nu'uanu in contact with the enemy. Ka'iana, occupying the left of line, is killed while taking shelter behind a wall at this location.

that Ka'iana and his warriors took their turn at holding off the advancing enemy.[58] The location was certainly never intended for anything more than a brief stand, the ancient stronghold at La'imi so tantalizingly close, just one mile further up the valley.[59]

There are mixed accounts of precisely how it occurred, but the critical event at 'Elekōkī was the mortal wounding of Ka'iana.[60] Whether he was killed by spear, ball, shrapnel or stone fragment is rather immaterial as compared to the overall impact of his death.[61] A fearless warrior and charismatic leader, his loss inflicted an incalculable blow to the morale and tactical leadership of the allies at a critical juncture in the battle.

Although not expressly relevant to the outcome of the battle, there is an especially poignant story in connection with the action at 'Elekōkī.[62] It relates to Ka'iana's wife, Kekupuohi, who remained loyal to Kamehameha after her husband's defection.[63] One of the noted wahine ali'i proficient in the use of firearms, according to this interpretation, Kekupuohi accompanies the attacking vanguard and is present when her husband's stricken body is obtained and brought back to the Hawaiian lines. Kekupuohi, rather famously, comforts Ka'iana in his dying moments.[64]

G FORMER HEIAU OF KAWĀNANAKOA AT MAUNA 'ALA

Suggested Vantage Point:

- The Royal Mausoleum has formal hours and terms of admittance.

Mauna 'Ala. Location of the Royal Mausoleum and former heiau of Kawānanakoa. Here, Ka'iana's body was offered up in traditional sacrifice. The flora we see today is dramatically different from what was present in 1795. *(iStockphoto LP)*

This photo of the Royal Mausoleum was taken shortly after construction of the chapel in 1865. Note the limited vegetation along the flanking ridge. Photo by H.L. Chase, circa 1868-1872. *(Hawaiian Historical Society photo)*

A heiau existed below Alapena on the site of the present Royal Mausoleum.[65] The heiau is seized after a short fight. As customary, Kaʻiana's body is offered at the heiau as a sacrifice to Kamehameha's war god, Kūkaʻilimoku. Evidently, the Hawaiians continue to press the advance even while offering up Kaʻiana. Things turn from bad to worse for the allies. During the withdrawal, Kaʻiana's brother, Nāhiʻōleʻa, is killed outright and Kalanikūpule is gravely wounded.

Unable to continue in command, Kalanikūpule withdraws from battle in the vicinity of a luakini heiau (an especially exalted place of worship) near present-day Jack Lane, located in the former ʻili of Niolopa. The last mōʻī of Oʻahu is evacuated together with his personal retinue over the ridge at Alewa.[66] With their senior leaders now mostly casualties of war, the surviving allied pūkaua forge on to the stronghold at Laʻimi.

H LA'IMI STRONGHOLD

Suggested Vantage Point:

- La'imi Road off the Pali Highway. Street parking.

La'imi, the proverbial bridge too far, is located beside Nu'uanu Stream in the former 'ili of Pū'iwa.[67] The allies reach its protective walls with their forces depleted, short on leadership, and badly demoralized. Some of the ordnance Ka'iana brought with him has probably made it as far as La'imi. By all accounts, the Hawaiians bring the accumulated power of their guns to bear at La'imi, perhaps for the first time. The overwhelmed garrison soon falls, some fleeing to a heiau at Pū'iwa. Surrender is not an option. Those that are able and know the trails scramble up the surrounding cliffs and away to safety.

The stronghold of La'imi in the vincinity of La'imi Road off the Pali Highway. The stronghold was located beside Nu'uanu Stream in the former 'ili of Pū'iwa. The allies reached its protective walls with their forces depleted, short on leadership, and badly demoralized. The Hawaiians brought the accumulated power of their guns to bear at La'imi and progressively reduced its defences.

BROOK Kapūkuniahi. PARKER© 2009

Without horses or field carriages to pull guns designed for shipboard use and weighing upwards of 250 pounds, the Hawaiians were forced to innovate, lashing their ordnance to sturdy sleds. *(Illustration © 2009 Brook Kapūkuniahi Parker)*

A typical naval carriage gun of the period. "6-pounder" refers to the weight of the iron shot. The gun itself weighs about 600 pounds.

◼ AHIPU'U STRONGHOLD

Suggested Vantage Point:

- Intersection of Ahipu'u Street and Pāhoehoe Place off the Pali Highway. The stronghold was located on the high ground in the distance. Street parking.

Ahipu'u stronghold located in the former 'ili of Waolani is situated beside Waolani Stream and is the main defensive for a complex of important heiau.[68] Like La'imi, it too falls to a concerted siege, adding to the growing despair of the defending force.

The intersection of Ahipu'u Street and Pāhoehoe Place off the Pali Highway. The stronghold of Ahipu'u was located on the high ground in the distance beside Waolani Stream. It was the main defensive works for the complex of important heiau at Waolani. Like La'imi, it fell to a concerted siege.

J PŪʻIWA

Suggested Vantage Point:

- Vicinity of Park Street and Pūʻiwa Road, *behind* Queen Emma Summer Palace. Free parking in the Nuʻuanu Valley Park parking lot.

- **Note:** There is a fee for admittance to Queen Emma Summer Palace and parking is for visitors only.

After the fall of Laʻimi and Ahipuʻu, the allies regroup as best they can at Pūʻiwa, employing a heiau for protection.[69] But it is just a matter of time before that too collapses. With the final defeat at Pūʻiwa, the back of the allied defensive is finally broken and the battle said to be well and truly lost.

Nuʻuanu Valley Park behind Queen Emma Summer Palace.

Pūʻiwa Road and Polohinano Place. After the fall of Laʻimi and Ahipuʻu, the allies re-grouped at Pūʻiwa employing a heiau near the stream for protection.

The shattered but determined remnants of the allied army, including family and retainers, beat a grueling retreat for over a mile and a quarter, following the course of the rock-strewn stream as far as the open wetlands known as Luakaha. The battle transitions into a series of desperate running engagements.

A NOTE ON THE VARIOUS NARRATIONS

Some narrations are quite adamant that Kalanikūpule continued the fight right up to the final encounter at Nuʻuanu Pali, where he is killed outright by a spear-thrust.[70] Other accounts portray the mōʻī dying of his wounds upon Mua heiau.

A mele about the battle asserts that the Hawaiian warriors rested at Pūʻiwa after a long day of fighting. It also suggests that the women accompanying Kamehameha's van then took up the fight with a body of Kalanikūpule's warriors that had taken up refuge in a heiau at the entrance to Waolani.[71]

Phase 5 – The Hasty Defense

KAHUAILANAWAI (VICINITY OF JACKASS GINGER POOL, LOWER LUAKAHA)

Suggested Vantage Point:
[see street map below]

- Off Nu'uanu Pali Drive near Reservoir Number Two. Limited off-street parking. A short hike along Judd Memorial Trail following Nu'uanu Stream.

- **Caution:** Frequent rains can cause the trail to become muddy and the rocks slippery. Wear appropriate footwear and bring mosquito repellent.

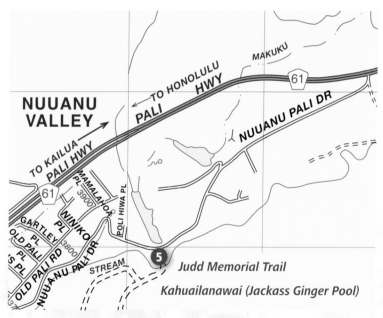

(David Phears, Phears Hawaii Maps)

Kahuailanawai (vicinity of Jackass Ginger Pool, Lower Luakaha) off Nu'uanu Pali Drive near Reservoir Number Two. The last stand of the combined O'ahu army at Kahuailanawai is perhaps the least known and least remembered events of the battle of Nu'uanu.

At Kahuailanawai in Lower Luakaha, near the place popularly known as Jackass Ginger Pool, the flanking ridge is not quite so steep. The allies might very well have expected to escape by cutting over the crest toward Mānoa, there to regroup and fight another day. What they find instead, to their undoubted dismay, is Kamehameha's flanking division coming down off the ridge, blocking the trail.[72]

With the Hawaiian flanking force crossing over from the back of Pauoa on one side, wetlands hemming them in on the other, and the main attacking force still driving up the valley, the last cohesive body of allied warriors form rank for one final superhuman effort. It is a holding action intended to provide a little extra time for their broken forces loved ones and followers to escape over the few accessible trails into neighboring valleys. But for these proud warriors, it is the end of the line.

The last stand of the combined O'ahu army at Kahuailanawai is perhaps the least known and least remembered action of the battle of Nu'uanu, their heroism eclipsed by later events at the Pali.

Koa engaged in close quarter fighting employing traditional weapons. *(Illustration © 2009 Brook Kapūkuniahi Parker.)*

Nuʻuanu viewed traveling up the Pali Highway from downtown Honolulu. Steep ridges flank both sides of the valley, converging in a narrow gap high up in the Koʻolau range. The ridge pictured below (Dowsett Highlands area) divides Nuʻuanu from neighboring Pauoa Valley.

Phase 6 – The Pursuit

NU'UANU PALI (NU'UANU PALI STATE PARK WAYSIDE)

Suggested Vantage Point:
[see streetp map below]

- Nu'uanu Pali Drive at Pali Highway. Be prepared for strong gusty winds and occasional wet weather!

- **Note:** There is a parking fee for non-residents.

The battle long since lost, the relentlessly pursued and disorganized remnants of the allied forces are canalized and pressed by their attackers back toward Nu'uanu Pali in small groups. No quarter is expected or given. The allies either fight to the death atop the crest or tumble headlong down the precipitous trail hunted by their determined foe. Some accounts refer to the defenders throwing themselves off the heights rather than face the indignity and humiliation of capture.

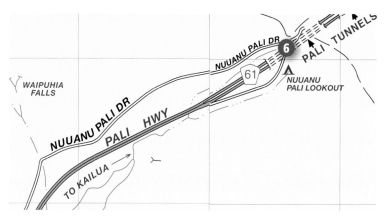

(David Phears, Phears Hawaii Maps)

Herb Kawainui Kāne's iconic portrayal of the fighting at Nu'uanu Pali. After the decisive action at Kahuailanawai the relentlessly pursued and disorganized remnants of the allied force are pressed by their attackers back toward Nu'uanu Pali in small groups. No quarter is expected or given. The allies fight to the death atop the crest or tumble headlong down the precipitous trail. Some throw themselves off the heights rather than face the indignity and humiliation of capture.

("The Battle at Nu'uanu Pali" © 2009 Herb Kawainui Kāne)

6

Nu'uanu Pali, looking windward.
(Douglas Peebles Photography)

The "Pali Notches"

Along the spine of the ridge approaching Nuʻuanu Pali are two "notches" that look to be manmade. Some narratives hold that these notches were the location of Kaʻiana's cannon.[73] It is a topic of much discussion and some accumulated romance. The notches have not been systematically studied to prove or disprove the story, but a quick review of the ground reveals several reasons why a commander would *not* select this location as a gun emplacement.[74] The reasons are largely technical:

- 6-pounder guns were short range weapons. Depending on the charge and wind direction, the maximum effective range of round shot (i.e., a cannon ball) was about 600 yards. The primary theater at Pūowaina and lower Nuʻuanu was close to six miles away.

The "notches" at Nuʻuanu Pali viewed from lower down the valley.

The Pali viewed from windward (or Koʻolaupoko), Oʻahu before construction of the Old Pali Road. Photo by H.L. Chase, circa 1868-1872. *(Hawaiian Historical Society photo)*

Hawaiians crossing Nuʻuanu Pali from the leeward or Honolulu side. Photo by H.L. Chase, circa 1868-1872. *(Hawaiian Historical Society photo)*

An aerial view of Nuʻuanu and Nuʻuanu Pali Road from the direction of windward, Oʻahu. 1931 photo by G.R. Hayman, 11th Photo Section, US Army Air Corps.
(Hawaiian Historical Society photo)

- The simple iron or bronze guns in use at the time fired on a flat trajectory. Owing to the extreme elevation, any round shot fired from the notches is likely to have splashed straight down into the ground without rolling or ricocheting (the usual method of inflicting damage on the enemy).

- Following the discharge or muzzle flash of slower velocity weapons (particularly older well-worn ones), round shot could often be observed in flight. Troop movements could be adjusted accordingly. Guns situated atop a more or less fixed platform, on the other hand, had correspondingly limited flexibility.

- With only two guns to alternate, it might be possible to fire one round per minute without respite, but then the danger of a premature cook off was very real—a danger accentuated by the absence of any dependable water source at the notches.

The Pali today, as viewed from windward, O'ahu.

While the notches offer an undeniably commanding view of the valley (and windward O'ahu), the technology required to effectively exploit that location would not have been available to Ka'iana, even had he managed the Herculean task of hauling the guns up there. A far more likely explanation for the presence of the notches is that they are the remnant of some long forgotten observation post or early warning beacon. It is also possible that the report from cannon fired atop the notches served merely as an effective alarm to those lower down the valley. Their true purpose will likely remain a mystery until such time a proper study is conducted.

Aftermath and Assessment

In the collection of the Bishop Museum are two kāhili, magnificent feather standards and traditional symbols of royalty, with a strong connection to the battle of Nuʻuanu. The kāhili incorporate the partial remains of Kaʻiana, Kalanikūpule and Kaneoneo, who died "in or as a result of the battle of Nuʻuanu in 1795."[75]

There are no definitive numbers on casualties, but conservative estimates are that the Hawaiian forces lost fewer than one hundred in the battle of Nuʻuanu, the allies anywhere from four to eight hundred. The actual figure is probably much higher. Many more lives were almost certainly lost in the mopping-up operation after the battle. "In those days, prisoners of war, if of high rank, were sacrificed on the temple altars; if they were commoners, they faced death and physical desecration."[76] The hardships imposed on Oahuans were intensified by the practice of land re-allocation and colonization by the victors. Great families were often made destitute and their genealogies erased from public memory. Kamehameha had a large army on Oʻahu to feed which imposed heavy demands on an already burdened agriculture, resulting in near famine conditions.[77] A sagacious leader, Kamehameha realized that he must do something quickly to restore productivity.[78] The ahupuaʻa of Nuʻuanu, with its many streams and conducive climate, must have seemed an obvious place to start, only it took some months to re-establish.

By most accounts, Kalanikūpule escaped defeat, living as a fugitive for several days or weeks until he was captured near Waipiʻo and sacrificed by Kamehameha at the Diamond Head heiau of Papaʻenaʻena.[79] One brother, Koalaukane, escaped Kamehameha's clutches (for a second time) to live out the remainder of his life on Kauaʻi.

Nuʻuanu, as it turns out, was the last great battle of any comparable scale to be fought within the Islands. Although it significantly contributed toward the process of permanent unification, strictly speaking, Nuʻuanu did not settle the matter. The Hawaiians, after all, had succeeded in taking other islands before, only to relinquish them. After Nuʻuanu, a state of war existed for another five years between what could (for the first time) be called the "Hawaiian Islands" and Kauaʻi. Kamehameha, moreover, had to contend with a variety of threats to his authority, including a rebellion at home, foreign incursions, losses from disease and natural disaster.

With the peaceful submission of Kauaʻi in 1810, Kamehameha ultimately succeeded in uniting the Islands, but could the kingdom endure beyond him? Following his death in 1819, the kingdom, in fact, seemed on the very brink of disintegration. Visiting German naturalist Adelbert von Chamisso went so far as to predict imminent collapse, with Kalanimoku succeeding Kamehameha's rule on Oʻahu,

Part of a 1910 pageant portraying the landing of Kamehameha at Waikīkī.
(Photo by Ray Jerome Baker. Hawaiian Historical Society photo)

Keʻeaumoku on Maui, Kaumualiʻi on Kauaʻi, and Liholiho on Hawaiʻi.[80] The irrevocable establishment of the Kamehameha dynasty (and permanent union) was not achieved through any single battle. It required sweeping social and administrative reforms, including elimination of the inherently destabilizing influences of the kapu system.[81] The battle of Kuamoʻo in December 1819, will forever be remembered as the "last stand" of the old religion, but of far larger significance is its status as the last major example of collateral challenge to authority by a junior hereditary line played out on the field of battle.

For kānaka, the battle of Nuʻuanu understandably conjures up mixed emotions, signifying as it does the end of one (or more) island nation's hopes for self-determination. At the same time providing a lasting reminder of the tremendous sacrifices made to forestall or bring about unification. Nuʻuanu can just as readily be seen to mark the birth of a new Hawaiian nation in the Pacific. Hawaiians, moreover, are intimately aware that the contestants facing one another at Nuʻuanu were, in many cases, very closely related: brothers, cousins, nephews. Clearly, the difference between "Oahuan" and "Hawaiian," was more of an accident of birth or geography more than anything else. Lineage and fealty, irrespective of birthplace, was a much more significant matter. And although pain and suffering are natural by-products of warfare (often poignantly conveyed in Hawaiian mele), war was simply one of the ways that Hawaiians selected their leadership, an integral aspect of mana and utterly inseparable from their belief system. Hawaiians went to war, for the most part, willingly and purposefully, unburdened by any great sense of guilt or tragedy.

In 1897 the Republic of Hawaii awarded a government contract to build a formal road over the pass at Nuʻuanu Pali, known today as the "Old Pali Road." During construction, one of the chief engineers, John Henry Wilson, claimed to have uncovered the skeletal remains of several hundred individuals at the base of the precipice, understandably attributed to Kalanikūpule's fallen warriors. Construction was not halted, however, and "rock blasted from the cliffs, obliterated this historic, natural cemetery."[82]

Hawaiians commemorate the battle of Nuʻuanu each April at the Pali in a solemn ceremony, continuing a tradition that began at least a century ago. Nuʻuanu Pali, "the place of Great Decision," naturally serves as a focal point for this stirring memorial, for only atop the Pali is it possible to grasp in one single breathtaking view the journey, the sacrifice, the accomplishment, and dream of 1795.[83]

Selected reasons for the Hawaiian success at Nuʻuanu:

- Careful timing

- Overwhelming numbers (required to defeat an entrenched enemy)

- Assiduous preparations for invasion including development of an adequate arms cache

- Staged amphibious assault on neighboring islands to secure the "back door" and replenish supplies; applying a "scorched earth" policy to West Maui in order to prevent further support from reaching Kalanikūpule

- Secure lines of communication

- Careful reconnaissance, intelligence gathering and adjustment to plans upon landing

- Divisional approach to troop deployment

- Concentration of limited firepower

- Good use of harassing fire to demoralize and canalize the enemy

- Effective flanking maneuver

- Surgical removal of enemy defensive position via special operation (alleged gun emplacements atop the dominating ridge)

- Relentless and energetic pursuit of the enemy's forces once engaged

Strategic and tactical miscalculations contributing to the allied defeat:

- Following the combined Kaua'i and Maui defeat at the battle of Kepuwaha'ula'ula (March 1791), the allies maintain a large standing army on the Hawai'i-facing shores of Maui. This sustained effort sapped the resources of the extended Maui kingdom, greatly handicapping Kalanikūpule's ability to prepare for war

- Inability to co-opt an earlier rival, Kā'eokūlani, when this may have tipped the balance of power against Kamehameha

- Ill-conceived betrayal and murder of Captain William Brown, eliminating a valuable ally (and an effective deterrent), giving encouragement to the enemy

- No attempt to obstruct the enemy's amphibious assault

- Over-reliance on a static forward defense at Pūowaina

- Failure to partition the enemy's superior forces into manageable encounters, reducing the enemy's concentration and momentum

- Failure to provide adequate reserves or concealed forces to pursue windows of opportunity

- Failure to secure the flanking ground

- Failure to neutralize the enemy's tactical assets (i.e., artillery)

Suggested Driving Route

You can create your own self-guided tour of the battlefield by combining the Battlefield Study contained in this book with the following driving instructions. The suggested route does not include stops at the locations of the old heiau that used to be located at the base of Punchbowl Crater, which is a heavily trafficked area, or Papakōlea. These five sites, however, can be easily observed from atop Punchbowl. Allow three hours for the entire trip. For ease of use, the Hawaiian diacritical marks have been omitted from the directions to correspond with most street maps and signs.

Begin your tour at Diamond Head Crater. From the lookout located in front of the Kāhala Tunnel entrance to Diamond Head State Monument, view the area from Kāhala to Wai'alae (Phase 1, beachhead for the Hawaiian invasion).

Driving Directions:

1. From downtown Honolulu, travel on H1 East.

2. Exit 26A (Koko Head Avenue) and make a right turn off of the freeway, onto Koko Head Avenue.

3. Turn left at Pahoa Avenue.

4. Make a right turn at 18th Avenue. Follow 18th Avenue, past Kapi'olani Community College, noting the view of the bay.

5. At Diamond Head Road, make a right turn.

6. Make an immediate left turn and head up the entrance road to Diamond Head State Monument.

7. Just in front of the tunnel entrance, turn left into the small parking lot.

   - **Note:** There is a fee for parking inside the crater.

After Diamond Head Crater, travel downtown to Punchbowl Crater, location of many of the sites of Phase 2 and 3 of the battle.

Driving Directions:

1. Exit the Diamond Head State Monument.

2. Turn left at Diamond Head Road.

3. Turn right at Makapuu Avenue.

4. Turn left onto Alohea Avenue.

5. Continue onto 6th Avenue.

6. Turn left at Harding Avenue.

7. Turn left at 5th Avenue, onto H1 West.

8. Exit 24A for Wilder Avenue. Follow Wilder through the Makiki neighborhood for just over one mile.

9. Turn right on Piikoi Street. Follow the curve in the road.

10. Turn right on Pensacola Street. Follow Pensacola until it becomes Auwaiolimu Street.

11. From Auwaiolimu, turn left on Hookui Street, just after the overpass.

12. Turn left on Puowaina Drive.

13. Follow Puowaina to the National Memorial Cemetery of the Pacific, also known as Punchbowl. Park near the path heading up to the Observation Point, located on your left as you enter the Memorial Cemetery.

From the Observation Point, take note of the following sites:

- **Thomas Square**
- **Kānelā'au heiau**, where Alapai Street intersects with Kinau and Lunalilo Streets.
- **Mauna heiau**, behind Queen's Medical Center near Lusitana and Lauhala Streets.
- **Kahehūnā heiau**, vicinity of Royal School, where Punchbowl and Lusitana Streets intersect.

- **Kaʻakopua heiau**, vicinity of Central Middle School, where Queen Emma Street and Vineyard Boulevard intersect.

Drive past the Memorial and Chapel. Park near the gap in the haole-koa hedge. Pauoa and Papakōlea can be viewed from the crater rim. Next, travel to the battle-related sites of Phase 4.

Driving Directions:

1. Exit the National Memorial Cemetery of the Pacific.

2. Follow Puowaina around to the other side of the crater.

3. Turn right on San Antonio Avenue.

4. Turn right on Lusitana Street.

5. Turn left on Pauoa Road, continuing through the highway underpass.

6. Turn right on Nuuanu Avenue.

7. Park on or near South Judd Street. ʻElekōki once stood near South Judd Street and the Craigside development.

8. Further up Nuuanu Avenue on your right side is the Royal Mausoleum, where the former Kawānanakoa heiau stood.

9. Continuing up Nuuanu Avenue, Jack Lane, where Kalanikūpule is alleged to have quit the battle, is on your left.

10. Further up the road on the right is Laimi Road, vicinity of Laʻimi stronghold.

11. Next, on the left off Nuuanu Avenue, is Ahipuu Street, vicinity of Ahipuʻu stronghold.

12. Still proceeding up Nuuanu Avenue, make a right turn onto Puiwa Road, vicinity of the allied defeat at Pūʻiwa. Park in the Nuuanu Valley Park parking lot.

To reach the vicinity of Phase 5, the last stand at Kahuailanawai:

1. Exit Nuuanu Valley Park and turn right on Nuuanu Avenue.

2. Turn right on Nuuanu Pali Drive and proceed.

3. Park on the shoulder near the bridge, immediately past the sharp 'S' curve in the road (at the Judd Memorial Trail trailhead).

Finally, proceed to Phase 6, site of the final clash at Nuʻuanu Pali:

1. Continue on Nuuanu Pali Drive.

2. Turn right on Pali Highway.

3. Follow the highway up to the Pali. Exit at Nuʻuanu Pali State Wayside, noting the "notches" atop the ridgeline as you proceed up the road.

4. At the Lookout be sure to read the commemorative plaque to the battle.

- **Note:** There is a parking fee for non-residents.

A view entering Nuʻuanu Pali State Park Wayside looking up the valley toward the "Pali notches."

Summary of Vantage Points

*Please keep off private property, park your vehicle responsibly, and respect the privacy of neighborhood residents – *Mahalo*

(1) Lēʻahi (Diamond Head Crater)

- From Diamond Head Road take the entrance road up to Diamond Head State Monument.

- Turn left into the small parking lot located just *in front* of the tunnel entrance. Free short-term parking.

- **Note:** There is a fee for parking inside the crater.

(2) Thomas Square

- Community park at intersection of South King Street and Victoria Street. Street parking.

(3) Former Kānelāʻau Heiau

- The intersection of Alapaʻi Street and Kīnaʻu Street below the Lunalilo Freeway. Street parking.

(4) Former Mauna Heiau

- Just above Queen's Medical Center near Lusitana Street and Lauhala Street. Street parking.

(5) Former Kahehūnā Heiau

- Vicinity of Royal School at Punchbowl Street and Lusitana Street. Street parking.

(6) Former Kaʻakopua Heiau

- Vicinity of Central Middle School at Queen Emma Street and Vineyard Boulevard. Street parking.

(7) Pūowaina or "Punchbowl" (National Memorial Cemetery of the Pacific)

- Enter from Pūowaina Drive. The cemetery has formal hours. No entrance fee or parking fees.

(8) Papakōlea

- Papakōlea Community Park. Located at the intersection of Tantalus Drive and Kauhane Street. Street parking. **Watch for children at play!**

(9) 'Elekōkī (Vicinity of "Craigside")

- Between South Judd Street and Craigside Place off Nu'uanu Avenue. Street parking.

(10) Former Heiau of Kawānanakoa at Mauna 'Ala

- The Royal Mausoleum has formal hours and terms of admittance.

(11) La'imi Stronghold

- La'imi Road off the Pali Highway. Street parking.

(12) Ahipu'u Stronghold

- Intersection of Ahipu'u Street and Pāhoehoe Place off the Pali Highway. The stronghold was located on the high ground in the distance. Street parking.

(13) Pū'iwa

- Vicinity of Park Street and Pū'iwa Road, behind Queen Emma Summer Palace. Free parking in the Nu'uanu Valley Park parking lot.

- **Note:** There is a fee for admittance to Queen Emma Summer Palace and parking is for visitors only.

(14) Kahuailanawai (Vicinity of Jackass Ginger Pool, Lower Luakaha)

- Off Nu'uanu Pali Drive near Reservoir Number Two. Limited off-street parking. A short hike along Judd Memorial Trail following Nu'uanu Stream.

- **Caution** – frequent rains can cause the trail to become muddy and the rocks slippery. Wear appropriate footwear and bring mosquito repellent.

(15) Nu'uanu Pali (Nu'uanu Pali State Park Wayside)

- Nu'uanu Pali Drive at Pali Highway. Be prepared for strong gusty winds and occasional wet weather!

- **Note:** There is a parking fee for non-residents.

Endnotes

[1] Early missionaries referred to the garden-like valley opposite the harbor at Honolulu as "Anuanu."

[2] The precise number is impossible to ascertain. Estimates placing Kamehameha's forces at 12,000 and the allied defenders at 9,000 are entirely reasonable if oral histories, population estimates and mobilization methods are utilized in combination. The contribution of auxiliaries drawn from the makaʻāinana – the general populace – plus retainers and camp followers may account for some of the discrepancy in estimates. Sahlins puts the number between 10,000 and 15,000. Sahlins, *Anahulu*, 41.

[3] Stewart, *The United States Army*, vol. 1. Under Thomas Jefferson (1800-1807), the regular army was further reduced to 3,287 officers and men (two infantry regiments, one artillery regiment and a small corps of engineers).

[4] Only four on record during the year 1795 – The *Union, Jane, Ruby* and *Mercury*.

[5] Historian Samuel Kamakau, and others, assert that Kamehameha and Kalanikūpule, for example, were actually half-brothers. Kamakau, *Ruling*, 188.

[6] The term *mōʻī* is probably of more recent derivation, a more or less equivalent term for "king." *Aliʻi nui* (high chief) or *aliʻi ai moku* (island chief) are often substituted.

[7] Readers are advised to consult the suggested list of readings for a detailed history on Kamehameha's birth and rise to power.

[8] At the battle of Kaheʻiki. The Maui victory over Oʻahu was followed by the brutal repression of a rebellion, virtually eliminating the ancient lines of senior Oahuan nobility. Kahekili also seized Molokaʻi from the Oahuan dynasty.

[9] Nowhere was this more evident or critical than on Oʻahu. Kalanikūpule was, in comparison to his father, a popular ruler. But the defeat of Kāʻeokūlani earned him, for example, only lukewarm support from the districts of Waialua and Waiʻanae, which had supported his erstwhile rival.

[10] "Kepaniwai." Reference to the damming of streams with the bodies of fallen warriors is sometimes used as a figure of speech in Hawaiian tradition to emphasize an especially costly and sanguinary clash of arms. Strictly speaking, it is accurate as a matter of degree, but should not be taken too literally in all cases. Standing on the rim of ʻĪao Valley, it is easy to see how this might actually have been possible. The same metaphor has been used in conjunction with the battle of Nuʻuanu in reference to the action at Kahuailanawai.

[11] Kāʻeokūlani's decision to turn on his nephew, Kalanikūpule, at the insistence of his supporters (having just repudiated war) is illustrative of a not insignificant point—mōʻī did not always enter into large endeavors entirely of their own volition. It is, therefore, more useful and perhaps more accurate to attribute such bold undertakings as the assembling of a great armada to the combined will of the Hawaiian leadership, not just the unilateral decree of Kamehameha.

[12] The battle of ʻAiea, or Kukiʻiahu, December 12, 1794.

[13] Kamehameha's ambitions were made very clear early on (circa 1790), when the Hawaiian leader famously sent an embassy to Kahikili preparing the way for an invasion of Oʻahu. Instead, Kahikili pressed Kamehameha for an armistice to continue for the duration of his life. Kamakau, *Ruling*, 150, and Cordy, *Exalted*, 332.

[14] The schooner *Jackal* (or sometimes "Jackall") and sloop *Prince Lee Boo* under direction of Captain William Brown. The capacity of these two vessels for inflicting great damage was vividly demonstrated for Kalanikūpule at the battle of ʻAiea. Kalanikūpule certainly had not sufficient wherewithal (in terms of trade goods) to entice Brown into supporting him in yet another risky venture. Brown already faced the likelihood of an inquest into the accidental death of John Kendrick, captain of the *Lady Washington*. The Oʻahu leader's immediate objective remains unclear. It is suggested in many narratives that he intended to sail with the *Jackal* and *Prince Lee Boo* to Hawaiʻi along with a small fleet in order to "make war on Kamehameha." Kamakau, *Ruling*, 170. Realistically, a surprise attack was his only hope of success. It is also possible that Kalanikūpule intended to sail for Maui in hope of leveraging whatever prestige and influence his mana (and his commandeered ships) could garner to raise a fresh force against Kamehameha. Kalanikūpule's plans, whatever they might have been, were dashed by the quick thinking of the first mates of the *Jackal* and *Prince Lee Boo*, George Lamport and William Bonallack.

[15] Constructed with the assistance of George Vancouver.

[16] There are many versions of what happened next, mostly transmitted through oral histories and reinterpreted through the (not always subtle) lens of Missionary-influenced chroniclers. Witnesses were rarely, if ever, key players in the events that took place at Nuʻuanu. Moreover, these chroniclers often had no clear understanding of military practice or theory, employing terms like battalion, company and division interchangeably.

[17] Pearl Harbor is the only Hawaiʻi battlefield listed in the National Register of Historic Places. The first plaque commemorating the battle was placed at the Pali in 1907 by the Daughters of Hawaiʻi. Now missing, the tablet inscription read: "Erected by the Daughters of Hawaiʻi – 1907 – to Commemorate the Battle of Nuuanu, Fought in this Vicinity – 1795 – when the Invading Conqueror, Kamehameha, Drove the Forces of Kalanikupule, King of Oahu, to the Pali, and Hurled Them Over the Precipice,

thus establishing the Kamehameha Dynasty." The memorial was donated by H.J. Heinz. of "packer" fame. *Honolulu Advertiser*, 29 Mar. 1953.

[18] John Young and Isaac Davis are perhaps the best known of these adventurers, attaining ali'i nui status in later years. Noted historian Samuel Kamakau refers to them as "leaders in his [Kamehameha's] wars," but does not specifically impute independent command to them at the battle of Nu'uanu. Kamakau, *Ruling*, 147. Young and Davis apparently operated under the command of Ke'eaumoku according to Abraham Fornander, *An Account*, 326.

[19] The masters of visiting merchant vessels traded firearms for supplies as early as 1786. Ka'iana, it is often asserted, accumulated a considerable cache of arms following his return from the Orient (1788) and to have placed these weapons at the disposal of Kamehameha. Miller, *Ka'iana*, 10. By 1787, "The principal chiefly concern quickly became securing supplies of firearms and the knowledge of how to use them effectively," notes Galois (*Colnett*, 63). "It is unclear whether Colnett [Captain James Colnett of the *Prince of Wales*] began the trade in firearms on the Hawaiian Islands, but he certainly contributed to its development."

[20] A primary example, written dispatches between commanders with orders that could not be easily intercepted or misinterpreted. It is also possible that foreign retainers contributed after a fashion to the mana of ali'i nui.

[21] Sahlins, *Anahulu*, 43. Gowen, *Napoleon*, 240, includes Isaac Davis and Peter Anderson as having "charge of the cannon."

[22] According to some narratives, the English crews were able to deliver to Kamehameha the firearms that would otherwise have been deployed against his own warriors. In other accounts they only deliver a warning message to Young and Davis in a brief letter. Almost certainly, the surviving crews of the *Prince Lee Boo* and *Jackal* required reprovisioning before sailing for China, as this was not their intended destination when departing O'ahu. Since the additional store of weapons placed in the holds by Kalanikūpule was at hand, this would have made an expedient item for barter. It is doubtful the crews, under the circumstances, would have lingered off the shores of Hawai'i for long. Daws provides a very nice summary of all the sources relating to Lamport and Bonallack's letter to Young, Daws, *Century*, 357 *ff.*

[23] Sahlins, *Anahulu*, 43. Cordy, *Exalted*, 331, asserts that "Kamehameha's first peleleu fleet" was deployed in 1790 for the invasion of Maui, but this date seems too early. While a small number of swivel guns may have been mounted to the bows of Kamehameha's flagships, it would be several more years before true peleleu of heavier and larger design with sails modeled after Western vessels would be produced in any significant numbers.

[24] For example, Kauwahine, Kahekili's wife is said to have participated in the battle of Kaheʻiki on Oʻahu in 1783. Kamakau, *Ruling*, 136.

[25] The foremost advocate of this interpretation was historian Stephen Desha. See Desha, *Kekūhaupiʻo*, 409-410. Muskets, in particular, would have afforded wahine aliʻi a means of participating in battle removed from the rigor and protocols of close quarter fighting.

[26] This name is also frequently applied to the battle of Kapaniwai at ʻĪao Valley.

[27] See Kamakau, *Ruling*, 172.

[28] By 1795, the Island of Kahoʻolawe was reduced by warfare to a largely barren and unpopulated territory.

[29] Kaʻiana was descended from Maui chiefs on his mother's side and the senior Keawe line (from Hawaiʻi) on his father's side. He fled Oʻahu for Kauaʻi after being implicated in the failed uprising against Kahikili in 1785-86. One of the first aliʻi to go abroad, he left Kauaʻi in 1787, traveling to India and then China, returning to Hawaiʻi the following year having amassed a great deal of overseas experience. Cordy, *Exalted*, 330. Kaʻiana was said to rival Kamehameha for ambition and ego. Fornander, *An Account*, 344.

[30] Stephen Desha, *Kekūhaupiʻo*, 407-408, provides the most convincing figures for the number of forces deployed (with a few caveats) based on historical comparisons and known mobilization methods. His reference to "five kāuna" is undoubtedly a misinterpretation and should read "five kaʻau." The typical company sized unit or organization was forty, not four. The stated breakdown of each division is a rough approximation for the purposes of analysis.

[31] There are contradictory references to Boki and Kaneoneo (of Kauaʻi) serving as senior pūkaua in command of the allied forces.

[32] According to one account, Kaʻiana's men were mostly from Puna, veteran's of his earlier (unsuccessful) campaign against Keōua (1790). If Kaʻiana had been left in charge of the rear division, as is sometimes suggested, it would account for his ability to slip away from the fleet without much difficulty. As his betrayal dawned on the Hawaiians waiting for his arrival at Maunalua Bay, their anger and indignation, in all likelihood, grew steadily. Newell, *Kaméhaméha*, 351-353.

[33] Sahlins, *Anahulu*, 36.

[34] There was a long history of conflict between the two polities, dating back at least as far as Kamalālāwalu's invasion of Hawaiʻi, circa 1650.

[35] The impoverished state of agricultural production meant that Kalanikūpule had little to offer visiting ships in the way of trade. Notably, George Vancouver was appalled by the intensity of the effort to obtain arms in the Islands and would have nothing to do with it. See Note 19 on James Colnett, above.

[36] Winne, "Music," 200.

[37] Paki, *Legends*, 88.

[38] The absence of any determined opposition isn't altogether surprising. The Maui rulers of Oʻahu resided at Kailua and Kāneʻohe, located on the windward side of the island. The general preference and custom was for so-called battles of convenience. Earlier battles on Oʻahu had led to the development of strongholds within the heartland valleys.

[39] Probably at Kahaloa. The (Western) vessels and peleleu in the Hawaiian fleet with larger drafts would have steered clear of the shallow reefs along Maunalua Bay, preferring the deeper and better-charted waters off Waikīkī. Kamakau thoughtfully addresses some of the considerations for selecting a battle site on Oʻahu (*Ruling*, 150), accounting somewhat for the principal landing within sight of Koko Head.

[40] Kaʻiana is both a noble and tragic figure, much venerated in Hawaiian tradition. His legendary defection is included in all the major sources and much too involved to relate in summary. See Miller, *Kaʻiana*, for a well constructed and recent biography of Kaʻiana.

[41] Following the battle of Kepuwahaʻulaʻula (circa 1790), Kahekili posted the equivalent of a large standing army on the Maui coast facing Hawaiʻi for the better part of three years. The supply requirements of this army constituted a huge drain on the extended Maui realms, made worse by the Kukiʻiahu War between Kalanikūpule and Kāʻeokūlani. Sahlins, *Anahulu*, 40-41.

[42] The Kona district was renamed "Honolulu" in 1859. Sterling, *Sites*, 257.

[43] Bergin, *Honolulu Advertiser*, 24 Sept. 1950.

[44] Pūowaina was an ancient place of sacrifice. Westervelt, *Legends*, 19.

[45] The British employed a more or less similar tactical arrangement using Martellos well into the 1840s.

[46] Indeed, the majority of Hawaiian casualties for the entire battle were probably received at the foot of Pūowaina. "Here the battle raged the fiercest" says Emma Metcalf Nukuina (*Pacific Commercial Advertiser*, 29 Jun. 1909).

[47] Sometimes identified as "Mana" heiau.

[48] Some narratives suggest the actual location is *above* the freeway, perhaps in the vicinity of Dole Park.

[49] Nukuina identifies the Hawaiian pūkaua in charge of this flanking operation as Heulu. Nukuina, *Pacific Commercial Advertiser*, 29 Jun. 1909.

[50] If (military) history offers us any lesson at all, it is that the breakthrough at Papakōlea was achieved by means of a night assault. But this is pure speculation.

[51] Nukuina identifies Kaomealani as the young son of Kalanikūpule. Nukuina, *Pacific Commercial Advertiser*, 29 Jun. 1909.

[52] An ahupua'a was a form of political land division that typically ran from the highlands to the sea. Some sources do *not* define Nu'uanu as an autonomous ahupua'a. Instead they regard Nu'uanu Valley and Nu'uanu Pali (overlooking the 'okana of Ko'olaupoko) as comprising the upper or highland extension of the ahupua'a of Kou (Honolulu). This may be just a matter of chronology, reflecting reforms undertaken after the battle.

[53] Pali simply means "cliff," any cliff. Ancient Hawaiians knew this spot between the peaks of Lanihuli and Kōnāhuanui by a much less clinical description. They called it Kaholeakeahole, a poetic reference to the stripping effect of the winds.

[54] For an analogous picture of the agricultural prehistory of Nu'uanu, see Kirch, *Anahulu*, 23.

[55] Paki, *Legends*, 17. See also Sterling, "Kawa'luna Heiau" in *Sites*, 304. McAlllister, *Archaeology*, 84-85 and Beckwith, *Mythology*, 301. Westervelt relates other fascinating tales of Waolani. Westervelt, *Legends*, 20.

[56] See Sterling, "Haipu and Ahipuu" in *Sites*, 300.

[57] Also spelled 'Alekoki. 'Ili have no precise equivalent in English. They are technically a "subdivision" of an ahupua'a, somewhat analogous to a precinct.

[58] This was either a terrace wall or, as some suggest, part of a heiau complex. See Raphaelson, *Honolulu Star-Bulletin*, 17 Jan. 1925.

[59] Very little has been done to investigate the Nu'uanu battlefield as such. Wolforth notes, "The paucity of forts in the Hawaiian archaeological record may be a function of our not recognizing them on the landscape." Wolforth, *Manifestations*, 10 and 18.

[60] In some accounts, Ka'iana is killed at La'imi rather than at 'Elekōkī.

[61] John Young recalled that Ka'iana was killed by a spear. Lisiansky, *Voyage*, 132.

[62] Again, in some accounts, this event occurred at La'imi.

[63] Miller, *Ka'iana*, 14-16, implies that Ka'iana may have had more than one wife. Gowen, *Napoleon*, 244, suggests that "husband and wife decided to remain on opposite sides so that defeat of the one side or the other would not entirely obliterate the hope of mercy."

[64] Desha, includes Kekupuohi's lamentation chant in his version of Ka'iana's final moments. Desha, *Kekūhaupi'o*, 411.

[65] Raphaelson, *Honolulu Star-Bulletin*, 17 Jan. 1925.

[66] Kalanikūpule, in some traditional accounts, is said to have made a farewell speech in which he thanks his commanders for their valor and bids them to do what they can to save as many as possible.

[67] There appears to have been an 'ili by the same name ("La'imi") a little further up the valley during the 19th century.

[68] Clarice Taylor defines this location as "La'imi Iki," placing La'imi, Ahipu'u and Pū'iwa a little further up the valley in the vicinity of Nu'uanu Drive above Dowsett Avenue. See Taylor, *Honolulu-Star Bulletin*, 6 Jun. 1953.

[69] The name Pū'iwa literally means to shy away, suggesting the fear and desperation of those who took refuge there in the face of certain disaster. The name was most likely given to the location *following* the battle.

[70] "The natives still point out the spot where the king of the island stood, when he hurled his last spear at the advancing foe, and received the fatal wound; and many, as they pass by, turn aside from the path, place their feet on the identical spot where he is said to have stood." Ellis, *Narrative*, 27. Bingham, *Residence*, 47 ff, attributes a nearly identical story to Ka'iana's footprints. Bergin, *Honolulu Advertiser*, 24 Sept. 1950, also places Kalanikūpule's death at the Pali.

[71] Raphaelson, *Honolulu Star-Bulletin*, 17 Jan. 1925.

[72] This was the division that had, early in the battle, climbed the ridge behind Papakōlea and made its way via Tantalus. Some narratives suggest that they were in possession of firearms and thus harassed the beleaguered allies.

[73] This contention is well articulated by Van James, *Ancient*, 30. James asserts that the Hawaiian forces were "hindered in their advance by two cannons Kalanikūpule had installed in the cliff in notches twelve feet deep and thirty wide … Kamehameha therefore sent a runner to Waikīkī directing a small group of warriors to proceed up Mānoa Valley and over the sharp Kōnuahuanui Pali to remove the gun emplacements." For other theories about the notches, see Sterling, *Sites*, 314 and McAllister, *Archaeology*, 88.

[74] The author has personally hiked the location.

[75] National Park Service, *Register*, 1997. According to W.T. Brigham the kāhili incorporates the shinbone of Kaneoneo "a noted chief of Kaua'i who fell in the battle." The bones of Ka'iana and Kalanikūpule "honor the handle ... This use of human bones was considered honorable, while to use parts of the human framework for fish hooks, spear points, or to inlay spittoons was a deep injury to the dead." Brigham, *Handbook*, 14.

[76] Silva, *Kahuailanawai*, 8.

[77] Sahlins, *Anahulu*, 41.

[78] Sahlins credits the relatively quick return to productivity to two factors: the army of occupation departed O'ahu to put down a rebellion on Hawai'i, reducing demand, and to the competent administration Kamehameha left in place under Kuihelani. Sahlins, *Anahulu*, 41.

[79] Some narratives report that Kalanikūpule was sacrificed at a heiau in Moanalua.

[80] Kuykendall, *Hawaiian*, Vol. 1, 61.

[81] Other necessary reforms initiated by Kamehameha to solidify his rule included the deliberate disarming of ali'i retinues (the centralization of military force) and a new power-sharing arrangement with his inner circle of supporters. See D'Arcy, *Warfare*, for a well-articulated and informative discussion on the process of political centralization in Hawai'i.

[82] The blasting was carried out under the supervision of Joe Puni. Krauss, *Johnny*, 58.

[83] Paki, *Legends*, 86.

Bibliography and Further Reading

ANNON. *Ke Kaua o Nuʻuanu: he hoʻomanaʻo ʻelua haneli makahiki*. Alt. title, *The Battle of Nuʻuanu: A Bicentenary Commemoration, 1795-1995*. Windward Community College Pamphlet Collection. Honolulu: n.p., 1995.

BECKWITH, MARTHA. *Hawaiian Mythology*. Honolulu: University of Hawaiʻi Press, 1976.

BINGHAM, HIRAM. *A Residence of Twenty-One Years in the Sandwich Islands*. 3rd ed. Canandaigua, New York: H.D. Goodwin, 1855.

BROUGHTON, WILLIAM R. *A Voyage of Discovery to the North Pacific Ocean, 1795-1798*. Reprint of the London 1804 ed. New York: Da Capo Press, 1967.

BISHOP, CHARLES. *The Journal and Letters of Captain Charles Bishop*. Cambridge: Cambridge University Press for the Hakluyt Society, 1967.

BOIT, JOHN. *Log of the Union: John Boit's Remarkable Voyage to the Northwest Coast & Around the World 1794-1796*. Edmund Hayes, ed. North Pacific Studies, No. 6. Portland: Oregon Historical Society, 1981.

BRIGHAM, WILLIAM T. *A Handbook for Visitors to the Bishop Museum*. Honolulu: n.p., 1903.

CAMPBELL, SID. *Warrior Arts and Weapons of Ancient Hawaii*. Berkeley: Blue Snake Books, 2006.

COLNETT, JAMES. *A Voyage to the North West Side of America: The Journals of James Colnett*. Robert M. Galois, ed. Vancouver: University of British Columbia Press, 2004.

CORDY, ROSS. *Exalted Sits the Chief*. Honolulu: Mutual Publishing, 2000.

CORDY, ROSS. *The Rise and Fall of the Oʻahu Kingdom*. Honolulu: Mutual Publishing, 2002.

D'ARCY, PAUL. "Warfare and state formation in Hawaii: the limits on violence as a means of political consolidation." *The Hawaiian Journal of History* No. 6, 2003.

DAWS, GAVAN. *Honolulu: The First Century*. Honolulu: Mutual Publishing, 2006.

DESHA, STEPHEN L. *Kamehameha and His Warrior Kekūhaupi'o*. Frances N. Frazier, trans. Honolulu: Kamehameha Schools Press, 2000.

DRAEGER, DONN F. "On Stone Hand Clubs: Classical Hawaiian Martial Culture." A study prepared at the East-West Center for the Bernice P. Bishop Museum, 15 Jan. – 15 Jul. 1997.

DUKAS, NEIL BERNARD. *A Military History of Sovereign Hawai'i*. Honolulu: Mutual Publishing, 2004.

ELLIS, WILLIAM. *A Narrative of a Tour through Hawaii, or Owhyhee*. Reprint of the London 1827 ed. Honolulu: Mutual Publishing, 2004.

EMORY, KENNETH. "Warfare." Ancient Hawaiian Civilization. A series of lectures delivered at The Kamehameha Schools. Honolulu: Kamehameha Schools Press, 1933.

FITZSIMMONS, JAMES PATRICK. *Warfare in Old Hawai'i: The Transformation of a Polemological System*. Diss. University of Hawai'i, 1969.

FORNANDER, ABRAHAM. *An Account of the Polynesian Race: Its Origin and Migrations*. vol. 2. Reprint of the London 1880 ed. Rutland, Vermont: Charles E. Tuttle Co., 1969.

GOWEN, HERBERT H. *The Napoleon of the Pacific–Kamehameha the Great*. New York: Fleming H. Revell Co., 1919.

HIGA, LINCOLN. "The Battle of Nuuanu: April, 1795." U.S. Army Military History Institute. Background paper prepared by the 30th Military History Detachment, U.S. Army Reserve, Dec. 1992.

HIROA, TE RANGI (Peter H. Buck). *Arts and Crafts of Hawaii*. Section 10: War and Weapons. 1957. Honolulu: Bishop Museum Press, 1964.

IHARA, VIOLET K. "Life in Ancient Hawai'i: Warfare and Weapons." State of Hawai'i, Dept. of Ed., lecture demonstration. 1974. Bishop Museum Archives. Memorandum 5.

JAMES, ROB. "The Battle of Nu'uanu." Descriptive wall map. Honolulu: Kamehameha Schools Press. 2004.

JAMES, VAN. *Ancient Sites of O'ahu: A Guide to Hawaiian Archaeological Places of Interest*. Honolulu: Bishop Museum Press, 1991.

JARVES, JAMES JACKSON. *History of the Hawaiian or Sandwich Islands*. Boston: Tappan & Dennet, 1843.

JUDD, BERNICE. *Voyages to Hawaii Before 1860*. Enlarged and ed. by Helen Yonge Lind. Honolulu: University of Hawai'i Press, 1974.

JUDD, WALTER F. *Kamehameha*. Norfolk Island, Australia: Island Heritage, 1976.

KAMAKA, PAEA KEALII AI'A. From the Womb to the Tomb–King Kamehameha Paiea I. Kamuela, Hawai'i: n.p., 1966.

KALAKAUA, H.H.M. KING DAVID. "Kaiana, The Last of the Hawaiian Knights," in *The Legends and Myths of Hawaii*. R.M. Daggett, ed. Reprint of the New York 1888 ed. Honolulu: Mutual Publishing, 1990.

KAMAKAU, S. M. *Ruling Chiefs of Hawai'i*. Rev. ed. Honolulu: Kamehameha Schools Press, 1992.

KĀNE, HERB KAWAINUI. *Ancient Hawai'i*. Captain Cook, Hawai'i: Kawainui Press, 1997.

KENN, CHARLES W. "The Army and Navy of Kamehameha I." MS. US Naval Institute, Annapolis, MD, Nov. 1945. Hawaiian Historical Society.

KIRCH, PATRICK V. AND SAHLINS, MARSHALL. "The Anahulu Valley and Hawaiian Prehistory," in *Anahulu: The Anthropology of History in the Kingdom of Hawaii*. (Kirch) vol. 2. Historical Ethnography. Chicago: University of Chicago Press, 1992.

KOLB, MICHAEL J. AND DIXON, BOYD. "Landscapes of War: Rules and Conventions of Conflict in Ancient Hawai'i (and Elsewhere)." *American Antiquity,* 2002.

KRAUSS, BOB. *Johnny Wilson: First Hawaiian Democrat*. Honolulu: University of Hawai'i Press, 1994.

KUYKENDALL, RALPH S. *The Hawaiian Kingdom 1778-1854*. vol. 1. Honolulu: University of Hawai'i Press, 1968.

LISIANSKY, UREY. *A Voyage Round the World in the Years 1803 [etc]*. London: S. Hamilton, Weybridge, Surrey, 1814.

MALO, DAVID. *Hawaiian Antiquities*. Nathaniel B. Emerson, trans. 1898. Honolulu: Bishop Museum Press, 1976.

MCALLISTER, J. GILBERT. *Archaeology of Oahu*. Bernice P. Bishop Museum Bulletin Number 104. Honolulu: Bishop Museum Press, 1933.

MCKINZIE, EDITH KAWELO KAPULE. *An Original Narrative of Kamehameha the Great Written in Ka Na'i Aupuni (1905-1906) by Joseph Poepoe: Hawaiian Text with English Translation and Brief Comparative Reviews of Earlier Historical Biographers of Kamehameha I*. vol 1. Diss. University of Hawai'i, 1982.

MILLER, DAVID G. "Ka'iana, the Once Famous 'Prince of Kaua'i.'" *The Hawaiian Journal of History,* vol. 22, 1988.

MITCHELL, DONALD D. KILOLANI. *Resource Units in Hawaiian Culture*. Rev. ed. Unit 18: Warfare and Weapons. Honolulu: Kamehameha Schools Press, 1992.

NAKUINA, EMMA METCALF. "The Great Battle of Nuuanu," in *Hawaii, Its People, Their Legends*. Honolulu: Hawaii Promotion Committee, 1904.

NATIONAL PARK SERVICE. "Notice of Inventory Completion for Native American Human Remains from the Battle of Nu'uanu in the Possession of the Bernice Pauahi Bishop Museum, Honolulu, HI." Federal Register. vol. 62, no. 166, 27 Aug. 1997.

NEWELL, C.M. *Kaméhaméha The Conquering King*. New York: Puntam's Sons Knickerbocker Press, 1885.

PAGLINAWAN, RICHARD KEKUMUIKAWAIOKEOLA, ELI, MITCHELL, KALAUOKALANI, MOSES ELWOOD, AND WALKER, JERRY. *Lua: Art of the Hawaiian Warrior*. Honolulu: Bishop Museum Press, 2006.

PAKI, PILAHI. *Legends of Hawaii: Oahu's Yesterday*. Honolulu: Victoria Publishers, 1972.

SAHLINS, MARSHALL AND KIRCH, PATRICK V. "The Conquest Period, 1778-1812," in *Anahulu: The Anthropology of History in the Kingdom of Hawaii*. (Sahlins) vol. 1. Historical Ethnography. Chicago: University of Chicago Press, 1992.

SILVA, CAROL. "Kahuailanawai: Site of Kamehameha's Last Major Fight." *Historic Hawai'i*. Honolulu: Historic Hawai'i Foundation, May 1991.

STEENWYK, JASON VAN. "Napoleon of the Pacific." *Military History*. Apr 2000.

STERLING, ELSPETH P. AND SUMMERS, CATHERINE C. *Sites of O'ahu*. Honolulu: Bishop Museum Press, 1978.

STEWART, RICHARD W., ED. "The United States Army and the forging of a nation, 1775-1917," in *American Military History*. vol. 1. Washington, D.C.: U.S. Army Center of Military History, 2005.

THRUM, THOMAS G., ED. "The Battle of Nuuanu." *Thrum's Hawaiian Almanac and Annual, 1899*. Honolulu: n.p., 1899.

THRUM, THOMAS G., ED. "Tributes of Hawaiian Tradition: The Pali and Battle of Nuuanu." Revised from the *Hawaiian Annual and Hawaiian Folk Tales*. Chicago: A.C. McClurg & Co., 1920.

WESTERVELT, W.D. *Hawaiian Legends of Old Honolulu*. Boston: G.H. Ellis Press, 1915.

WINNE, JANE LANTHROP AND PRATT, HELEN, ED. "Music." Ancient Hawaiian Civilization. A series of lectures delivered at The Kamehameha Schools. Honolulu: Kamehameha Schools Press, 1933.

WOLFORTH, THOMAS R. "Searching for Archaeological Manifestations of Hawaiian Battles on the Island of Hawai'i." Honolulu: Scientific Consultant Services, Inc., n.d.

Related Newspaper Articles

"Battle of Nuuanu Pali." W.C. Bergin. *Hawaii Weekly and Polynesian* (supplement to *Honolulu Advertiser Sunday Magazine*), 24 Sept. 1950.

"Hawaii Daughters Observe Jubilee." *Honolulu Advertiser*, Sec. 4, 9:3, 29 Mar. 1953.

"Kings, Gods and Wars Along Oahu's Roads: Legend Lore of Kamehameha Highway." Rayna Raphaelson. *Honolulu Star-Bulletin*, 17 Jan. 1925.

"Scenic Pali is Site of Historic Island Battle." *Honolulu Advertiser*, 5:1, 1 Feb. 1949.

"The Battle of Nuuanu." Emma Metcalf Nakuina. *Pacific Commercial Advertiser*, 29 Jun. 1909.

"Kamehameha's Greatest Victory: Conquered O'ahu 158 Years Ago." Clarice B. Taylor. *Honolulu Star-Bulletin*, 6 Jun. 1953.

"The Battle of Nu'uanu." Jerry Walker. Pacific Worlds & Associates, Native Place. 2 Jan. 2010. <www.pacificworlds.com/nuuanu/native/native2.cfm>

"The Notches of Nu'uanu Pali." Gerard Jervis. *Honolulu Magazine*, Nov. 1982.

Index

About the Author

Neil Bernard Dukas was born in Ontario, Canada and joined the Canadian Army as a young man. He served in both Reserve and Active capacities with the Governor-General's Horse Guards, Princess of Wales' Own Regiment, Mobile Command Headquarters, and the Canadian Land Forces Command and Staff College.

Former Dean of Instruction at Heald College (Honolulu Campus), Dukas is a member of the Honor Society of Phi Kappa Phi and the National Coalition of Independent Scholars. He graduated from Queen's University (Ontario, Canada) in 1983 with a four-year degree in Political Studies. In 1999 he received a Master of Arts degree in Humanities from California State University, Dominguez Hills.

An avid hiker, conservancy advocate and horseman, Dukas continues to research and write on the military history of Hawai'i with an emphasis on the years prior to annexation.

Also by Neil B. Dukas

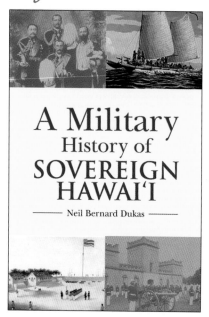

A Military History of Sovereign Hawai'i

An overview of Hawai'i's remarkable early military history, beginning with the classical period and progressing through to the annexation of Hawai'i by the United States.

ISBN-10: 1-56647-636-4 • ISBN-13: 978-1-56647-636-2
Trim size: 6 x 9 in • Page count: 240 pp
Binding: Softcover • Retail: $17.95

To order, visit **www.mutualpublishing.com**